Leckie
the education publisher
for Scotland

Higher
CHEMISTRY

T0340398

Revision + Practice
2 Books in 1

001/04032020

10 9 8 7

ISBN 9780008365264

Published by
Leckie
An imprint of HarperCollins*Publishers*
Westerhill Road, Bishopbriggs, Glasgow, G64 2QT
T: 0844 576 8126   F: 0844 576 8131
leckiescotland@harpercollins.co.uk   www.leckiescotland.co.uk

HarperCollins Publishers
Macken House, 39/40 Mayor Street Upper, Dublin 1 D01 C9W8 Ireland

Publisher: Sarah Mitchell
Project Manager: Gillian Bowman and Janice McNeillie

Special thanks to
Jess White (proofreading); Jouve (layout); Sarah Duxbury (cover design)

Printed by Ashford Colour Press Ltd

A CIP Catalogue record for this book is available from the British Library.

Acknowledgements

P10 © Dimedrol68 / Shutterstock.com; P31 Lorraine Kourafas / Shutterstock.com; P45 (left) Sergio Bertino / Shutterstock.com; (right) ifong / Shutterstock.com; P47 lucadp / Shutterstock.com; P49 MaraZe / Shutterstock.com; P57 (all images) ANDREW LAMBERT PHOTOGRAPHY / SCIENCE PHOTO LIBRARY; P60 Severe / Shutterstock.com; P62 BlueOrange Studio / Shutterstock.com; P64 (parsley) Evgeny Karandaev / Shutterstock.com, (thyme) Lukas Gojda / Shutterstock.com, (berries) margouillat photo / Shutterstock.com; P65 Daria Chichkareva / Shutterstock.com; P74 Paul Fleet / Shutterstock.com; P90 Maxal Tamor / Shutterstock.com; P122 MARTYN F. CHILLMAID / SCIENCE PHOTO LIBRARY; P128 Vinko93 / Shutterstock.com; P132 MARTYN F. CHILLMAID / SCIENCE PHOTO LIBRARY; P180 © Steve Lagreca / Shutterstock.com

This book contains FSC™ certified paper and other controlled sources to ensure responsible forest management.

For more information visit: www.harpercollins.co.uk/green

Contents

Contents

ebook

To access the ebook version of this Success Guide visit
www.collins.co.uk/ebooks
and follow the step-by-step instructions.

ANSWERS Check your answers to the practice test papers online:

www.collins.co.uk/pages/Scottish-curriculum-free-resources

Higher Complete Revision and Practice

Complete Revision and Practice

This **two-in-one Complete Revision and Practice** book is designed to support you as students of Higher Chemistry. It can be used either in the classroom, for regular study and homework, or for exam revision. By combining **a revision guide and two full sets of practice exam papers**, this book includes everything you need to be fully familiar with the Higher Chemistry course and exam.

About the revision guide

The revision guide covers the mandatory content in the key areas of the Higher Chemistry course.

The revision material is laid out over a double-page spread (sometimes four pages) in a clear, concise way. The main headings and sub-headings make it clear which part of the course is being covered. There are 'Top Tips' throughout which emphasise important points and give hints on how to answer questions. Each section has a Quick Test to enable you to self assess so that you know your areas of strength and areas you need to look at in more detail. Answers to each test can be found on pages 137–151. There is also a glossary, which gives you a quick and easy way to find explanations of key words and phrases found in the revision guide.

How to use the practice exam papers

This book contains two practice papers, which are modelled on the actual SQA exam as closely as possible in question style, level and layout. It is the perfect way to familiarise yourself with what the exam papers you will sit will look like.

The answer section which you can find online at *www.collins.co.uk/pages/Scottish-curriculum-free-resources*, contains worked answers to questions, letting you know exactly where the marks are gained in an answer and how the right answer is arrived at. It also includes practical tips on how to tackle certain types of questions, details of how marks are awarded and advice on just what the examiners will be looking for.

The practice papers can be used in one of two ways:

1. You can complete an entire practice paper under exam conditions and mark it using the answer section. If you complete a practice paper this way it is important to make a list of all the key areas that you are having difficulty with by referring to the topic index on page 158, and concentrating your study time on these areas before attempting the next practice paper.

2. You can use the topic index to tackle a key area one at a time. This allows you to focus on specific key areas that you particularly want to revise. It also allows you to revise exam-style questions for just the topics you have covered.

Whichever way you use the papers you must do your revision first!

The Higher Chemistry course

Structure

The Higher Chemistry course is made up of the following areas:

- 1: Chemical changes and structure
- 2: Nature's chemistry
- 3: Chemistry in society
- 4: Researching chemistry

Course assessment

This takes the form of a question paper (exam) and an assignment.

The exam carries a total of 120 marks and is made up of two sections:

- Paper 1 (25 marks) comprising 25 multiple-choice questions
- Paper 2 (95 marks) which is made up of a mixture of restricted and extended-response questions.

The assignment is a written report based on your own investigations and research into a topic in the course. It is marked out of 20, but scaled up to 30 to give it more weighting towards your overall grade.

Preparation for both of these is critical to getting the best grade possible in your Higher Chemistry course.

Leckie
the education publisher
for Scotland

Higher
CHEMISTRY

Revision Guide

Bob Wilson

Periodicity 1

The first 20 elements

Elements on the periodic table are arranged in order of increasing atomic number across a period (row). This allows chemists to make accurate predictions of physical properties and chemical behaviour for any element, based on its position in the periodic table. The similarities between the elements within a group (vertical column) arise because they have the same number of electrons in the outer energy level (shell). This similarity in the electron arrangement leads to a **periodicity** (repeating pattern) in the properties of elements.

The first 20 elements can be used to illustrate periodicity.

Metals: Atoms in a metal are held together by metallic bonding, an electrostatic attraction between positive nuclei and **delocalised electrons**.

Monatomic elements: the noble gases (group 0)

TOP TIP

London dispersion forces are very weak, but the more electrons there are in the atom, the bigger the London dispersion force. As a result, as you go down group 0, the melting and boiling points of the elements increase, as more energy is needed to separate the atoms.

At the far right of the periodic table we find the noble gases in group 0. Both their group name and number indicate a lack of reactivity. They are **monatomic** – they exist as individual atoms.

Each noble gas atom has a full outer energy level, and so does not need to react to achieve this. However, the noble gases are liquefied by lowering the temperature, which indicates there must be some force of attraction between the atoms, which is significant at a lower temperature but not at room temperature. These forces of attraction are known as **London dispersion forces**. They are caused by the continual movement of electrons in an atom, which causes a temporary uneven distribution of charge at opposite sides of an atom. This is known as a temporary dipole. This means that one side of the atom is temporarily slightly negative (δ^-), resulting in the other side being temporarily slightly positive (δ^+). This in turn induces a temporary dipole in a neighbouring atom. This results in the δ^- side of one atom attracting the δ^+ side of a neighbouring atom, so a force of attraction is formed between them.

TOP TIP

London dispersion forces exist in molecular substances, not only between the atoms of noble gas elements.

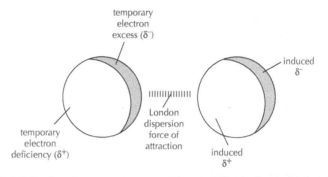

Diatomic elements: H_2, N_2, O_2, F_2 and Cl_2

TOP TIP

It is important to realise that when a molecular substance melts or boils, it is the weak London dispersion forces between molecules (**intermolecular forces**) which are broken, and not the strong covalent bonds holding the atoms together in the molecule.

Diatomic elements exist as two atoms covalently bonded.

Most are gases at room temperature that are easily liquefied at low temperatures. Bromine is a liquid, and iodine a solid at room temperature. This indicates that there are forces of attraction between the molecules. London dispersion forces attract the molecules to each other. However, in some of the molecules, these forces are so small that there is enough energy at room temperature to overcome the weak force of attraction and separate the molecules from each other. This is why most of the diatomic molecules are gases. Bromine and iodine are bigger molecules, and have more electrons than the smaller gas molecules. Therefore, the London

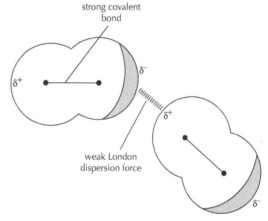

dispersion forces are much stronger between their molecules, and it takes more energy to separate them. This explains why they exist as a liquid and a solid at room temperature.

Quick Test 1

1. A student writing about noble gases stated: 'Helium is a gas which exists as individual atoms with weak forces of attraction between the atoms.' Describe fully the force of attraction acting between the atoms of noble gases.

2. (a) Describe the trend in melting points and boiling points of the halogens as you go down group 7 of the periodic table.

   (b) Explain the trend you described in (a).

Periodicity 2

Bigger molecules: P_4, S_8 and fullerenes (C)

Phosphorus and **sulfur** exist as solids with low melting and boiling points. Phosphorus exists as P_4 molecules, and sulfur as S_8 molecules. The atoms which make up the molecules are held together by covalent bonds, and the molecules are held together by London dispersion forces. Due to the size of the molecules, there are more electrons than there are in, for example, diatomic molecules.

P_4: m.p. = 44°C
b.p. = 280°C

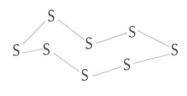

S_8: m.p. = 115°C
b.p. = 445°C

Therefore the London dispersion forces are stronger. This means at room temperature, there is not enough energy to break the forces and separate the molecules, so the elements are solid.

Carbon had, for a long time, been thought only to exist in the form of graphite and diamond, which are covalent networks (see page 11). However, in the 1980s, a molecular form of carbon was discovered. The molecule had 60 carbon atoms (C_{60}) and was named Buckminsterfullerene, often shortened to **fullerene**. Subsequent larger fullerene molecules have been made. Fullerenes are comprised of a series of carbons arranged in hexagons and pentagons. These are joined to make a ball shape. Fullerenes can also exist as tube shapes, often called nanotubes.

Like all covalent molecular elements, the molecules in fullerenes are held together by London dispersion forces. Because the molecules are so large, a lot of energy is required to separate them. Fullerene sublimes (changes from solid to gas) at around 600°C.

Models of ball-shaped fullerenes.

Covalent network elements: B, C (as diamond and graphite) and Si

Some non-metal elements have extremely high melting and boiling points. This indicates that there must be forces other than London dispersion forces holding their structures together. This can be seen in the elements **carbon**, **silicon** and **boron**.

Diamond and graphite (C)

Until molecules of fullerene (C_{60}) were discovered in the 1980s, it was thought that carbon only existed as giant **covalent networks**, in the form of diamond and graphite. Diamond and graphite are formed naturally by the combined action of heat and pressure deep under the Earth's crust.

In **diamond**, each carbon atom is covalently bonded to four other carbon atoms in a tetrahedral arrangement. All the outer electrons in the atom of each carbon are used to make single covalent bonds with neighbouring atoms. This results in a giant covalent network. There are no individual molecules in a network, nor are there unbonded (delocalised) electrons in the diamond structure. Therefore the diamond is a non-conductor of electricity.

—— strong bond

The structure of diamond.

The covalent network structure of **graphite** shows that any one carbon atom is bonded to only three other carbon atoms, unlike diamond where it is four. The diagram of the structure of graphite shows that the atoms form hexagonal plates, which are held together by weak London dispersion forces. These layers are able to slide over each other, so powdered graphite can be used as a lubricant.

------ weak attractive forces

Because each carbon atom only uses three of its outer electrons for bonding, the fourth electron is delocalised. It can move through the structure in a similar fashion to the delocalised electrons in metals. This explains why graphite is a good conductor of electricity.

The internal structure of graphite, showing carbon atoms joined in layered hexagonal plates, which are held together by London dispersion forces.

Melting and boiling points

In order to separate the atoms in a covalent network, the strong covalent bonds have to be broken. This requires a lot of energy, and explains why elements with covalent network structures have high melting and boiling points.

Silicon (Si) and boron (B)

Silicon is in group 4 of the periodic table. It has similar properties to diamond, in that it has a very high melting point, is extremely hard, and in its pure state is a very poor conductor of electricity. Silicon forms four covalent bonds with four other silicon atoms, and forms a covalent network similar to diamond.

Boron is similar to carbon in its ability to form stable covalent networks. Boron is a very hard, black material with a high melting point of above 2000°C.

TOP TIP

Diamond and graphite are unusual, in that rather than melting when heated to very high temperatures, they sublime. Sublimation is the transition of a substance directly from the solid to the gas phase, without passing through an intermediate liquid phase.

Quick Test 2

1. Explain why sulfur has a higher melting point than phosphorus.

2. Fullerenes are molecular forms of carbon which exist as solids that sublime (solid → gas) at temperatures approximately 600°C and above. Describe the intramolecular and intermolecular forces present in fullerenes, and state why their sublimation temperatures are so high.

3. Explain fully the following observations:

    (a) Diamond's sublimation point is much higher than sulfur's boiling point.

    (b) Graphite conducts electricity but diamond doesn't.

    (c) Silicon has many properties similar to diamond.

Periodicity 3

Covalent radius

The **covalent radius** can be used as a measure of the size of an atom.

The covalent radius is taken as half the distance between the nuclei of two atoms joined by a single covalent bond.

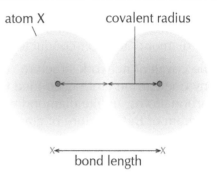

atom X   covalent radius

bond length

Change in covalent radius

Covalent radius decreases across a period →						
Li 134	Be 129	B 90	C 77	N 75	O 73	F 71

Covalent radius increases down a group

Na 154	Going **down a group**, there is an increase in atomic number, i.e. the number of protons in the nucleus. This is also means that the number of electrons in each atom increases. The number of electron shells occupied increases, and the inner electron shells screen the outermost electrons from the full pull of the positive nucleus. This means the outer electrons can move further from the nucleus.
K 196	
Rb 216	Going **across a period**, the atomic number increases by one each time, so the number of protons in the nucleus increases by one. At the same time, each atom gains an electron but in the same shell. There is no increased screening effect from the inner shells of electrons. Thus, as the atomic number increases across a period, the electrons in the outer shell are more strongly attracted to the nucleus, and so the covalent radius decreases.
Cs 235	

Ionisation energy

The **first ionisation energy** is the energy required to remove one mole of electrons from one mole of atoms in the gaseous state. Ionisation energy is measured in kJ mol^{-1}. The first ionisation energy for potassium for example, can be written as:

$$K(g) \rightarrow K^+(g) + e^-$$

Change in first ionisation energy

First ionisation energy generally increases across a period						
Li 520	Be 900	B 801	C 1086	N 1402	O 1314	F 1681

First ionisation energy generally decreases as you go down a group

Na 496	As you go **down a group**, the covalent radius of the atoms increases, i.e. the atoms get bigger. This means that the outer electrons are further away from the pull of the nucleus. Additionally, the number of filled electron energy levels increases, and they screen the outer electrons from the pulling effect of the nucleus. A combination of both effects makes it easier to remove an outer electron from an atom as you go down a group.
K 419	
Rb 403	As you go **across a period**, although electrons are being added, it is to the same energy level. The nuclear charge increases and the electrons are held more tightly, so it becomes harder to remove an outer electron from an atom.
Cs 376	

It is possible to remove two or more electrons from an atom. The second ionisation energy is the amount of energy required to remove a second mole of electrons.

Using calcium as an example:

First ionisation energy: $Ca(g) \rightarrow Ca^+(g) + e^-$ $\Delta H = +590$ kJ mol^{-1}

Second ionisation energy: $Ca^+(g) \rightarrow Ca^{2+}(g) + e^-$ $\Delta H = +1145$ kJ mol^{-1}

Second ionisation energies are always higher than first, because although electrons are being removed, the number of protons in the nucleus remains the same. Therefore, the pull on the remaining electrons is increased.

The total amount of energy required to remove two moles of electrons is the first ionisation energy and second ionisation energy added together, i.e. +1735 kJ mol^{-1} for Ca.

TOP TIP

In energy terms, it is not possible for atoms of group 2 elements to form a 3+ ion. This is because it would mean removing a third electron from an energy level closer to the nucleus, which requires too much energy.

Electronegativity

Electronegativity is the attraction an atom involved in a bond has for the electrons of the bond. Scientist Linus Pauling devised a scale, assigning numbers to elements based upon how electronegative that element is.

- Fluorine is the most electronegative element, and has a value of 4·0.
- Francium is the least electronegative, and has a value of 0·8.

The difference in electronegativity values of bonded atoms gives a good indication of the type of bonding that primarily exists between them. (See 'The bonding continuum', page 17.)

Change in electronegativity

	Electronegativity values increase across a period ⟶						
	Li 1·0	Be 1·5	B 2·0	C 2·5	N 3·0	O 3·5	F 4·0

Electronegativity values generally decrease — down a group ↓

Na 0·9	As you go **down a group**, the covalent radius increases and the outer electrons get further from the nucleus. The number of screening shells of electrons also increases. These factors combine and result in the nucleus having less of an attraction for the bonding electrons. Although the nuclear charge increases considerably going down a group, the bonding electrons are far from the nucleus and screened.
K 0·8	
Rb 0·8	As you go **across a period**, the covalent radius decreases and the number of screening shells of electrons stays the same, so the attraction the nucleus has for the bonding electrons increases. The nuclear charge increases across a period, so there are more protons able to attract the bonding electrons.
Cs 0·8	

TOP TIP

Covalent radii, ionisation energies and electronegativity values can all be found in the SQA data booklet.

Quick Test 3

> **Word bank**
>
> covalent, decreases, group, increases, nucleus, period, radius, screening, stronger

1. Complete the following paragraph, using the word bank to help you.

   As you go down a (i) _____ in the periodic table, the covalent
   (ii) _____ increases. This is because the number of screening
   shells of electrons (iii) _____ and the attraction between the
   (iv) _____ and the outermost electrons (v) _____.
   Going across a (vi) _____ the (vii) _____ radius decreases.
   This is because although the number of electrons increases, the number of
   (viii) _____ shells of electrons is the same. This means the attraction
   of the nucleus for the outermost electrons gets (ix) _____.

2. This table shows ionisation energy values (in kJ mol^{-1}) for a mole of magnesium
   atom forming ions:

first	second	third
738	1451	7733

   (a) Write equations to represent the first and second ionisation energies of magnesium.

   (b) Explain why there is an increase in the ionisation energy from first to second.

   (c) Explain why there is such a large difference between the second and third
   ionisation energy values.

   (d) Calculate the total energy required for a mole of gaseous magnesium atoms to form
   a mole of magnesium 2+ ions.

> **Word bank**
>
> across, covalent, decreases, down, electrons, nucleus, radius, screening, stronger

3. Complete the following paragraph, using the word bank to help you.

   As you go (i) _____ a group in the periodic table, electronegativity
   (ii) _____. This is because the covalent (iii) _____ and
   number of screening shells of (iv) _____ increase, and the attraction
   between the (v) _____ and the outermost electrons decreases.
   Going (vi) _____ a period the (vii) _____ radius decreases.
   This is because although the number of electrons increases, the number of
   (viii) _____ shells of electrons is the same. This means the attraction
   of the nucleus for the outermost electrons gets (ix) _____.

Structure and bonding 1

Types of bonding

Covalent – pure and polar

Covalent bonds are formed when non-metal atoms share pairs of electrons and the positive nuclei of each atom are held together by their common attraction for the shared electrons. When two atoms share bonding electrons equally, it is known as **pure covalent** bonding. This is because they have the same attraction for the bonding electrons – both atoms have the same **electronegativity** value (see page 14).

The bonds between chlorine atoms in a chlorine molecule (Cl_2) and phosphorus and hydrogen atoms in phosphine (PH_3) are pure covalent bonds.

$$Cl \overset{\bullet}{\underset{x}{\rule{1.2cm}{0.4pt}}} Cl \qquad P \overset{\bullet}{\underset{x}{\rule{1.2cm}{0.4pt}}} H \qquad \text{x and} \bullet = \text{bonding electrons}$$

Electronegativity value: $3{\cdot}0 \;-\; 3{\cdot}0$ $2{\cdot}2 \;-\; 2{\cdot}2$
(Difference = 0)   (Difference = 0)

Most covalent compounds are formed between elements with different electronegativity values. This means that one atom has a greater attraction for the bonding electrons than the other. The atom with the greater attraction for the bonding electrons will have a slightly negative charge (δ^-), leaving the other atom with a slightly positive charge (δ^+). A **permanent dipole** is formed. Bonding in which there is a permanent dipole is known as **polar covalent** bonding (polar bonding). The H–Cl bond in hydrogen chloride and the O–Cl bond in dichlorine monoxide are examples of polar covalent bonds.

$$H^{\delta+} \overset{\bullet}{\underset{x}{\rule{1.2cm}{0.4pt}}} Cl^{\delta-} \qquad O^{\delta-} \overset{\bullet}{\underset{x}{\rule{1.2cm}{0.4pt}}} Cl^{\delta+} \qquad \text{x and} \bullet = \text{bonding electrons}$$

Electronegativity value: $2{\cdot}2 \;-\; 3{\cdot}0$ $3{\cdot}5 \;-\; 3{\cdot}0$
(Difference = 0·8)   (Difference = 0·5)

Not all polar bonds are the same strength. The difference in electronegativity values gives a measure of how polar a bond is. As a general rule, if the difference in electronegativity is less than 2 the bond is covalent. The nearer the difference is to 2, the more polar covalent a bond is. The nearer the difference is to zero, the less polar covalent the bond is. (See 'The bonding continuum' on page 17.)

Fluorine is the most electronegative element, with a value of 4·0. When bonded with hydrogen with a value of 2·1, the difference in electronegativity is 1·9. This means that the covalent bond is extremely polar.

Ionic bonding

Differences in electronegativity values greater than 2 indicate that the electron movement from the atom of the element with the lower electronegativity value to the atom of the element with the greater electronegativity is complete, resulting in the formation of ions. Ionic compounds exist as giant lattices in which the oppositely charged ions attract each other. The electrostatic attraction between the positive ions and the negative ions is not in any particular direction, as is the case with covalent bonds. Ionic formulae give the simplest ratio of each type of ion in the substance. Sodium chloride and caesium chloride are ionic.

Both compounds have an electronegativity difference greater than 2·0 and so are ionic, but CsCl is slightly more ionic than NaCl because it has the bigger electronegativity difference between the elements.

○ Cl⁻ ○ Na⁺   ○ Cl⁻ ○ Cs⁺

TOP TIP

Caesium is the least electronegative element and fluorine the most electronegative. Caesium fluoride is considered to be the most ionic compound because the difference in electronegativity is the highest possible (3·2).

TOP TIP

Beware of assuming all metal/non-metal compounds are ionic. For example, the properties of tin(IV) chloride show a lot of covalent character, which would be expected from the difference in electronegativity value between the two elements, which is 1·2.

The bonding continuum

The idea of a **bonding continuum** can be used to give a more realistic indication of the bonding in a compound. The bonding continuum has ionic bonding at one end and pure covalent bonding at the other end, with polar covalent bonding in between. The numbers in the diagram are the difference in electronegativity between the bonded atoms.

3·0	2·0	1·5	1·0	0·0
Li^+F^-	$Be^{2+}(F^-)_2$	$C^{\delta+} \!-\! F^{\delta-}$	$N^{\delta+} \!-\! F^{\delta-}$	$F \!-\! F$
ionic		polar covalent		pure covalent
X^+Y^-		$X^{\delta+} \!-\! Y^{\delta-}$		$X \!-\! Y$

TOP TIP

Although the difference in electronegativity is a useful indicator of bonding, it has to be combined with physical properties to be absolutely sure of the bonding present in a compound.

To say that bonding is on a continuum means that the type of bonding changes gradually as the difference in electronegativity between atoms increases. There is no sharp distinction between covalent and ionic bonds.

Quick Test 4

1. Use the electronegativity values in the SQA data booklet to predict the type of bonding which would predominate in the following compounds:

   (i) magnesium oxide; (ii) tin(IV) bromide; (iii) hydrogen iodide

   Justify each of your answers.

2. Explain the difference between pure covalent bonding and polar covalent bonding.

3. Explain what is meant by the bonding continuum.

Structure and bonding 2

Intermolecular forces

The **intermolecular forces** acting between molecules are known as **van der Waals forces**. Three types of van der Waals force are: **London dispersion forces**, **permanent dipole–permanent dipole interactions** including **hydrogen bonding**.

TOP TIP

Intermolecular forces exist between the **atoms** of monatomic elements (group 0) and the **molecules** of covalent molecular elements and compounds.

London dispersion forces

London dispersion forces are much weaker than all other types of bonding. They exist as a result of attractions between induced temporary dipoles. This is explained in **Periodicity 1** (pages 8 and 9).

Permanent dipole–permanent dipole interactions

Permanent dipole–permanent dipole interactions occur between **polar molecules**. A molecule is only polar if it has a slightly positive (δ^+) side and a slightly negative (δ^-) side. Polar molecules are said to have a permanent dipole.

Polar molecules

δ^+H — Clδ^-

δ^+ side of | δ^- side of
molecule | molecule

(hydrogen chloride)

δ^- side of molecule

$\overset{\delta^-}{O}$

$\underset{\delta^+}{H}$ $\underset{\delta^+}{H}$ δ^+ side of molecule

(water)

TOP TIP

A molecule can contain polar bonds but the molecule need not necessarily be polar. The atoms in the molecule and its shape have to be considered.

Non-polar molecules

δ^-O=Cδ^+=Oδ^-

(carbon dioxide)

$\overset{\delta^-}{Cl}$

$\underset{}{C}\delta^+$

Cl$\underset{\delta^-}{}$ | Clδ^-
$\underset{\delta^-}{Cl}$

(tetrachloromethane)

The figures above clearly show that hydrogen chloride and water are polar molecules – they have a permanent dipole. Carbon dioxide and tetrachloromethane are non-polar molecules – they do not have dipoles. Both carbon dioxide and tetrachloromethane have a symmetrical shape, so the polarity of the bonds in a non-polar molecule cancel each other out and the molecules do not have a slightly negative (δ^-) side or slightly positive (δ^+) side.

As one end of a polar molecule is slightly negative, it can form an attraction with the slightly positive end of a neighbouring molecule. This is the permanent dipole–permanent dipole interaction. Although these forces of attraction are stronger than London dispersion forces they are still relatively weak. The diagram on the right shows the permanent dipole–permanent dipole interactions between trichloromethane molecules.

permanent dipole–
permanent dipole interactions

It isn't possible to tell by looking at two liquids if they are polar or not, but a simple experiment can be carried out to tell them apart:

TOP TIP

Permanent dipole–permanent dipole interactions are stronger than London dispersion forces for molecules with similar numbers of electrons. This results in polar substances having higher melting and boiling points than non-polar substances with similar numbers of electrons.

Polar substances, such as water, are attracted to a charged plastic rod but non-polar substances, like heptane, are not.

Quick Test 5

1. Bromine (Br_2) and iodine monochloride (ICl) have the same number of electrons yet iodine monochloride has a higher melting point.

    Explain this observation by reference to the type of intermolecular forces between the molecules.

2. (a) The shape of a PCl_3 molecule is shown:

    (i)   Describe the type of bonding between phosphorus and chlorine atoms in phosphorus trichloride (PCl_3).

    (ii) Is the molecule polar or non-polar?

    (iii) Justify your answer.

    (b) State what type of intermolecular force of attraction would predominate between PCl_3 molecules.

Structure and bonding 3

Hydrogen bonding

When hydrogen is bonded to the highly electronegative elements fluorine, oxygen and nitrogen, it results in the electrons in the bond being more strongly attracted away from the hydrogen atom. This would not be the case if other non-metal atoms were bonded to the hydrogen. The hydrogen atom is so small that the positive charge on the atom is unusually high and the bond is highly polar. This results in a very strong permanent dipole–permanent dipole interaction between molecules called a **hydrogen bond**.

Hydrogen bonds are the **strongest** of the van der Waals forces, and they cause some unusual and unexpected properties in compounds in which the hydrogen bonds are present.

Hydrogen fluoride (HF), water (H_2O) and ammonia (NH_3) are compounds with hydrogen bonds between their molecules. A diagrammatic representation of hydrogen bonding in water is shown below:

hydrogen bond

TOP TIP

Hydrogen bonding is a special type of permanent dipole–permanent dipole intermolecular attraction. It is the strongest van der Waals force and only occurs between molecules which have hydrogen bonded to oxygen, nitrogen or fluorine. Hydrogen bonds are weaker than covalent bonds.

The effects of hydrogen bonding

Boiling points and melting points

These graphs show the boiling points and melting points of the hydrides of the elements in groups 4 to 7:

- Groups 5, 6 and 7: NH_3, H_2O and HF have higher boiling points than other hydrides in their periodic group. This is because they have **hydrogen bonding** between their molecules. The molecules of the other hydrides in the groups are held together by permanent dipole–permanent dipole interactions and London dispersion forces, which are not as strong as hydrogen bonds. Therefore, less energy is required to separate them.

Boiling points of groups 4, 5, 6 and 7 hydrides

- Group 4 hydrides: the molecules are **non-polar** and are held together by weak London dispersion forces, which do not need much energy to separate them. As the molecules get bigger, they have more electrons, so the London dispersion forces increase. This in turn increases the boiling point of the compounds.

- The melting points show a similar trend, and can be explained in the same way.

Melting points of groups 4, 5, 6 and 7 hydrides

The properties of water

Hydrogen bonding also gives water some unusual properties.

Density

Water is unusual in that when it is cooled to 4°C it begins to **expand**. At its freezing point it is less dense than liquid water – this explains why ice cubes and icebergs float on water. It also explains why water pipes can burst in winter. When the water freezes and expands, the force causes the pipes to crack. This expansion of water is due to the ordering of the molecules into an open structure, with an increased number of hydrogen bonds. This is less dense than the arrangement of the molecules in liquid water.

Viscosity

The type of bonding present between molecules affects the viscosity (thickness) of a liquid. This can be demonstrated by dropping steel balls (released at the same time) through a variety of liquids.

- Diethyl ether is the least viscous of the liquids because it only has weak London dispersion forces holding molecules together.

- Ethanol has hydrogen bonding between molecules, so is more viscous than diethyl ether, but less viscous than water. Water has more highly polar –OH groups than ethanol, allowing more strong hydrogen bonds to form between water molecules than between ethanol molecules.

substance:	water	ethanol	diethyl ether
structure:	$\overset{\delta-}{O}$ with $\underset{\delta+}{H}$ $\underset{\delta+}{H}$	$\overset{\delta-}{O}$ with $\underset{\delta+}{H}$ C_2H_5	O with C_2H_5 C_2H_5
molecular mass:	18	46	74

steel ball

Solubility

Water's ability to dissolve a wide range of substances is due to the high polarity of the bonds within it. Water is particularly efficient at dissolving **polar** and **ionic** substances.

- Hydrogen chloride (HCl) exists as **polar** molecules. The polar covalent bond between the hydrogen and the chlorine breaks, and the resulting ions are attracted to the water molecules. The (aq) symbol is used to indicate that the ions are hydrated in solution:

$$H^{\delta+}(aq) + Cl^{-}(aq)$$

- Sodium chloride exists as an **ionic** lattice. The water molecules interact with the ions in the lattice, breaking the electrostatic attraction between the ions. The ions then go into solution. A force of attraction is created between the ions and the polar water molecules – the ions are hydrated with water molecules.

> **TOP TIP**
>
> To predict the solubility of a compound in water, the key features which need to be considered are:
> - the presence of hydrogen bonding
> - whether the shape of a molecule makes it polar.

- **Non-polar** substances like fats and oils cannot form strong intermolecular forces of attraction with water, and therefore are not dispersed throughout the water like soluble polar covalent and ionic substances. Non-polar solvents like tetrachloromethane can dissolve non-polar substances by forming London dispersion forces between the molecules.

> **TOP TIP**
>
> Polar covalent and ionic substances generally tend to be soluble in polar solvents, like water. Non-polar substances generally tend to be soluble in non-polar solvents.

Miscibility

Miscibility is the ability of liquids to mix in all proportions, forming a solution. Water and ethanol, for example, are miscible and this forms the basis for alcoholic drinks.

The water and ethanol molecules are both polar and they can hydrogen-bond with each other, which allows them to mix completely.

Oil and water are two liquids which are well known to be **immiscible** – they form two separate layers when mixed. Oil is non-polar, and so does not form forces of attraction with the polar water molecules. This means they separate when shaken together.

Quick Test 6

1. (a) Identify which of these compounds have hydrogen bonding between molecules:

    (i) HBr; (ii) NH_3; (iii) HF; (iv) CH_3OH

    (b) Justify your choices.

2. (a) This table shows the boiling points of the group 6 hydrides, and the number of electrons in a molecule of each compound.

Group 6 hydride	H_2O	H_2S	H_2Se	H_2Te
Number of electrons per molecule	10	18	36	54
Boiling point (°C)	100	−60	−41	−2

    (i) Based on the number of electrons in a molecule of each of the hydrides, what might the boiling point of H_2O have been predicted to be?

    (ii) Explain why the boiling point of H_2O does not follow the expected trend shown by the other group 6 hydrides.

    (b) When water freezes in pipes during the winter, it can cause them to burst. Explain what has happened to the water to cause this.

3. (a) Explain why potassium chloride dissolves easily in water but candle wax, which is a mixture of large hydrocarbon molecules, does not dissolve in water.

    (b) Heptane (C_7H_{16}) is a solvent that dissolves candle wax; it is a mixture of large hydrocarbon molecules. Explain why heptane can dissolve candle wax but water cannot.

Oxidising and reducing agents 1

Oxidation and reduction

Many chemical reactions involve electrons being lost by one 'particle' and gained by another. The 'particle' can be an atom, molecule or ion. These types of reaction are known as redox reactions. The particle losing electrons is said to be oxidised. The particle gaining electrons is said to be reduced. Ion–electron equations can be written for oxidation and reduction, and they can be added to form the redox reaction. Oxidation and reduction take place at the same time.

TOP TIP

Memory aid for what happens to the electrons:

Oxidation	**R**eduction
Is	**I**s
Loss	**G**ain

Elements as oxidising and reducing agents

Metals tend to act as reducing agents because they lose electrons easily.

Example

In the thermite reaction, iron(III) ions are reduced to iron atoms and aluminium atoms are oxidised to aluminium(III) ions. The liquid iron can be run off to repair cracks in things such as railway lines.

The iron(III) ions are reduced by gaining electrons from the aluminium atoms. The aluminium atoms are acting as **reducing agents**. When the aluminium atoms are oxidised and lose electrons to the iron(III) ions, the iron(III) ions are acting as **oxidising agents**.

TOP TIP

Reducing agents donate electrons in a reaction and are themselves oxidised. Oxidising agents accept electrons in a reaction and are themselves reduced.

Example

When green chlorine gas is bubbled through colourless potassium bromide solution, the solution turns orange. The bromide ions are displaced from solution and form bromine molecules. The chlorine molecules are reduced to chloride ions.

The chlorine molecules are acting as **oxidising agents** and are themselves reduced to chloride ions. The bromide ions are acting as **reducing agents** and are themselves oxidised to bromine molecules.

TOP TIP

Non-metal elements tend to act as oxidising agents because they accept electrons easily.

Reducing or oxidising agent?

Electronegativity values (see page 14) can be used to estimate whether an element is likely to be an oxidising or a reducing agent. Electronegativity is a measure of the attraction the atoms of an element have for electrons. The higher the value the greater the attraction for electrons i.e. form ions by gaining electrons. Fluorine, with a value of 4·0, will be a strong oxidising agent. The group 7 elements (halogens) are all strong oxidising agents.

The lower the electronegativity value, the more likely the element is to be a reducing agent i.e. form ions by losing electrons. The group 1 metals (alkali metals) have low electronegativity values and are strong reducing agents.

TOP TIP

Electronegativity values are found in the SQA data booklet.

Quick Test 7

1. Identify the oxidising and reducing agents in the following equations:

    (a) $Zn(s) + Cu^{2+}(aq) \rightarrow Zn^{2+}(aq) + Cu(s)$

    (b) $Br_2(aq) + 2I^-(aq) \rightarrow 2Br^-(aq) + I_2(aq)$

    (c) $Cr(s) + NiSO_4(aq) \rightarrow CrSO_4(aq) + Ni(s)$

Oxidising and reducing agents 2

Compounds as oxidising and reducing agents

Carbon monoxide (CO) is an example of a compound which can act as a **reducing agent**.

Iron is extracted from its ore in a blast furnace by reaction with carbon monoxide. Iron(III) ions are reduced to iron:

$$Fe_2O_3(s) + 3CO(g) \rightarrow 2Fe(\ell) + 3CO_2(g)$$

The compound **hydrogen peroxide** (H_2O_2) is one of the most powerful **oxidising agents**.

In acidic conditions, iron(II) ions are oxidised to iron(III) ions by hydrogen peroxide, which is itself reduced. Ion–electron equations can be written for the oxidation and reduction reactions, which can then be added to give the overall redox equation.

$$2Fe^{2+}(aq) \rightarrow 2Fe^{3+}(aq) + 2e^- \text{ oxidation}$$

$$\underline{H_2O_2(\ell) + 2H^+(aq) + 2e^- \rightarrow 2H_2O(\ell) \text{ reduction}}$$

$$2Fe^{2+}(aq) + H_2O_2(\ell) + 2H^+(aq) \rightarrow 2Fe^{3+}(aq) + 2H_2O(\ell) \text{ redox}$$

Working out ion–electron equations

The reduction equation for hydrogen peroxide is more complex than previous examples encountered. These more complicated ion–electron equations involve hydrogen ions and water molecules, and can be worked out as follows:

1. Write down the main reactant(s) and product(s) for the reduction/oxidation. Make sure there are the same number of each element (not oxygen) on each side of the equation.

2. Add water to one side to balance the oxygen.

3. Add $H^+(aq)$ to the other side to balance the hydrogen atoms.

4. Add electrons to the same side as the $H^+(aq)$ ions, so that both sides of the equation have the same charge.

Applying these rules to hydrogen peroxide being reduced (acting as an oxidising agent):

1. $H_2O_2(\ell) \rightarrow H_2O(\ell)$

   There are two hydrogens on each side so there is no need to balance.

2. The oxygen atoms are not balanced. Add another water molecule to the right-hand side: $H_2O_2(\ell) \rightarrow 2H_2O(\ell)$

3. Add two $H^+(aq)$ ions to the left-hand side to balance the hydrogen atoms: $H_2O_2(\ell) + 2H^+(aq) \rightarrow 2H_2O(\ell)$

4. Add two electrons to the left-hand side to balance the 2+ charge so that there is zero charge on both sides of the equation: $H_2O_2(\ell) + 2H^+(aq) + 2e^- \rightarrow 2H_2O(\ell)$

TOP TIP

Although you have to know how to write ion–electron equations, many of them are listed in the electrochemical series in the SQA data booklet.

Group ions as oxidising and reducing agents

The **permanganate ion** (MnO_4^-) and **dichromate ion** ($Cr_2O_7^{2-}$) are examples of group ions, which act as strong **oxidising agents** when in an acidic solution.

Example

Acidified potassium permanganate (potassium manganate(VII)) solution reacting with iron(II) sulfate

The iron(II) ions are oxidised to iron(III) ions.

$Fe^{2+}(aq) \rightarrow Fe^{3+}(aq) + e^-$ oxidation

The permanganate ions act as oxidising agents and are reduced to manganese(II) ions.

$MnO_4^-(aq) \rightarrow Mn^{2+}(aq)$ reduction

The ion–electron equation for the reduction reaction can be worked out using the balancing rules:

acidified $M_nO_4^-$ (aq)

Fe^{2+}(aq)

Mn^{2+}(aq) + Fe^{3+}(aq)

1. There is one Mn ion on each side so there is no need to balance.

2. The oxygens are not balanced so four H_2O need to be added to the right-hand side:
   $MnO_4^-(aq) \rightarrow Mn^{2+}(aq) + \textbf{4H}_2\textbf{O(ℓ)}$

3. Add eight $H^+(aq)$ to the left-hand side to balance the hydrogen atoms:
   $MnO_4^-(aq) + \textbf{8H}^+\textbf{(aq)} \rightarrow Mn^{2+}(aq) + \textbf{4H}_2\textbf{O(ℓ)}$

4. There is a total of 7+ charge on the left-hand side and 2+ on the right-hand side. Add five electrons to the left-hand side to balance the 2+ charge on the right:
   $MnO_4^-(aq) + \textbf{8H}^+\textbf{(aq)} + \textbf{5e}^- \rightarrow Mn^{2+}(aq) + \textbf{4H}_2\textbf{O(ℓ)}$

The two ion–electron equations can be combined to give the redox equation. The number of electrons in each ion–electron equation must be the same, so the oxidation equation must be multiplied by five:

$$5Fe^{2+}(aq) \rightarrow 5Fe^{3+}(aq) + 5e^- \text{ oxidation}$$
$$\underline{MnO_4^-(aq) + 8H^+(aq) + 5e^- \rightarrow Mn^{2+}(aq) + 4H_2O(ℓ) \text{ reduction}}$$
$$MnO_4^-(aq) + 8H^+(aq) + 5Fe^{2+}(aq) \rightarrow Mn^{2+}(aq) + 5Fe^{3+}(aq) + 4H_2O(ℓ) \text{ redox}$$

Note: The potassium and sulfate ions do not take part in the reaction – they are spectator ions.

Example

Acidified potassium dichromate reacting with tin(II) chloride

The tin(II) ions are reduced to tin(IV) ions.

$$Sn^{2+}(aq) \rightarrow Sn^{4+}(aq) + 2e^- \text{ oxidation}$$

The dichromate ions act as oxidising agents and are reduced to chromium(III) ions.

$$Cr_2O_7^{2-}(aq) + 14H^+(aq) + 6e^- \rightarrow 2Cr^{3+}(aq) + 7H_2O(\ell) \text{ reduction}$$

The two ion–electron equations can be combined to give the redox equation. The number of electrons in each ion–electron equation must be the same, so the oxidation equation must be multiplied by three:

$$3Sn^{2+}(aq) \rightarrow 3Sn^{4+}(aq) + 6e^- \text{ oxidation}$$

$$Cr_2O_7^{2-}(aq) + 14H^+(aq) + 6e^- \rightarrow 2Cr^{3+}(aq) + 7H_2O(\ell) \text{ reduction}$$

$$\overline{Cr_2O_7^{2-}(aq) + 14H^+(aq) + 3Sn^{2+}(aq) \rightarrow 3Sn^{4+}(aq) + 2Cr^{3+}(aq) + 7H_2O(\ell) \text{ redox}}$$

TOP TIP

The reduction ion–electron equations in the previous examples show the need for the oxidising agents to be acidified.

Example

Iodine in solution can be reduced by the sulfite ion:

TOP TIP

The **sulfite ion** (SO_3^{2-}) is an example of a group ion that can act as a **reducing agent**.

$SO_3^{2-}(aq)$

$I_2(aq)$

colourless solution containing $I^-(aq)$ and $SO_4^{2-}(aq)$

$$I_2(aq) + 2e^- \rightarrow 2I^-(aq) \text{ reduction}$$
$$SO_3^{2-}(aq) + H_2O(\ell) \rightarrow SO_4^{2-}(aq) + 2H^+(aq) + 2e^- \text{ oxidation}$$
$$\overline{SO_3^{2-}(aq) + H_2O(\ell) + I_2(aq) \rightarrow SO_4^{2-}(aq) + 2H^+(aq) + 2I^-(aq) \text{ redox}}$$

Note here that the number of electrons in each equation is the same, so the equations don't need to be multiplied up.

Although the oxidation equation for the oxidation of the sulfite ion can be found in the electrochemical series in the SQA data booklet, it can also be worked out by applying the four rules used previously:

1. $SO_3^{2-}(aq) \rightarrow SO_4^{2-}(aq)$

   There is one sulfur on each side, so there is no need to balance.

2. The oxygens are not balanced, so add one water to the left-hand side:

   $SO_3^{2-}(aq) + H_2O(\ell) \rightarrow SO_4^{2-}(aq)$

3. Add two $H^+(aq)$ to the right-hand side to balance the hydrogen atoms:

   $SO_3^{2-}(aq) + H_2O(\ell) \rightarrow SO_4^{2-}(aq) + 2H^+(aq)$

4. Add two electrons to the right-hand side to balance the 2+ charge:

   $SO_3^{2-}(aq) + H_2O(\ell) \rightarrow SO_4^{2-}(aq) + 2H^+(aq) + 2e^-$

Quick Test 8

1. Chlorine reacts with aqueous thiosulfate ions ($S_2O_3^{2-}$) which form sulfate ions (SO_4^{2-}). The unbalanced equation is shown:

   $$Cl_2(aq) + S_2O_3^{2-}(aq) \rightarrow Cl^-(aq) + SO_4^{2-}(aq)$$

   (a) Write the ion–electron equation for the reduction reaction.

   (b) Write the ion–electron equation for the oxidation reaction.

   (c) Combine the oxidation and reduction equations to give the balanced redox equation.

   (d) Identify the oxidising and reducing agents in the reaction.

2. In each of the following examples complete the ion–electron equations and state whether it is oxidation or reduction.

   (a) $S_4O_6^{2-}(aq) \rightarrow S_2O_3^{2-}(aq)$

   (b) $V^{3+}(aq) \rightarrow VO_3^-(aq)$

Oxidising and reducing agents 3

The electrochemical series

The electrochemical series lists various substances in order of how well they act as reducing/oxidising agents.

Part of the electrochemical series		
	Reaction	
	$Li^+(aq) + e^-$	$\rightleftharpoons Li(s)$
	$Cs^+(aq) + e^-$	$\rightleftharpoons Cs(s)$
	$Rb^+(aq) + e^-$	$\rightleftharpoons Rb(s)$
	$K^+(aq) + e^-$	$\rightleftharpoons K(s)$
	$Ca^{2+}(aq) + 2e^-$	$\rightleftharpoons Ca(s)$
	$Na^+(aq) + e^-$	$\rightleftharpoons Na(s)$
	$Br_2(\ell) + 2e^-$	$\rightleftharpoons 2Br^-(aq)$
	$O_2(g) + 4H^+(aq) + 4e^-$	$\rightleftharpoons 2H_2O(\ell)$
The strongest oxidising agents are at the bottom-left.	$Cr_2O_7^{2-}(aq) + 14H^+(aq) + 6e^-$	$\rightleftharpoons 2Cr^{3+}(aq) + 7H_2O(\ell)$
	$Cl_2(g) + 2e^-$	$\rightleftharpoons 2Cl^-(aq)$
	$MnO_4^-(aq) + 8H^+(aq) + 5e^-$	$\rightleftharpoons Mn^{2+}(aq) + 4H_2O(\ell)$
	$F_2(g) + 2e^-$	$\rightleftharpoons 2F^-(aq)$

The strongest reducing agents are at the top-right.

Using the electrochemical series

The electrochemical series can be used to predict whether a redox reaction will occur. Just looking at the substances involved alone gives no indication as to whether they will react.

The general rule is: if an oxidising agent is below the reducing agent in the electrochemical series, then a reaction will occur.

Example

Will potassium permanganate ($KMnO_4$) be able to oxidise bromide ions?

From the electrochemical series we see that MnO_4^- is bottom-left, and therefore is a strong oxidising agent (easily reduced); Br⁻ ions are above on the right-hand side, so the reaction will occur.

The ion–electron equations are obtained from the electrochemical series.

The permanganate ion is reduced so the equation is written as it is in the electrochemical series:

$$MnO_4^-(aq) + 8H^+(aq) + 5e^- \rightarrow Mn^{2+}(aq) + 4H_2O(\ell)$$

The bromide ions are on the right-hand side so the equation must be reversed:

$$2Br^-(aq) \rightarrow Br_2(aq) + 2e^-$$

Note that the potassium ion (K^+) is top-left in the electrochemical series so would not be able to act as a reducing agent – it is a spectator ion.

Using oxidising agents

Hydrogen peroxide is an extremely strong oxidising agent and acts as a very effective 'bleach' as it is able to break down coloured compounds. It is used to bleach wool, cotton and paper as well as lighten hair and even whiten teeth.

The strong oxidising power of **potassium permanganate** makes it useful in a number of areas, particularly as an antiseptic. Dilute solutions are used to treat mild skin conditions and fungal infections of the hands and feet, and can also cause some viruses to become inactive. Potassium permanganate is used in the water treatment industry to remove iron and hydrogen sulfide (rotten egg smell). It can be used in fish farms to kill parasites which infect the fish. Some florists use potassium permanganate for extending the life of fresh-cut flowers. It is also added for its disinfectant properties, as it can help to control algae spread in the water.

Quick Test 9

1. Look at the electrochemical series in the SQA data booklet and identify the strongest reducing agent and the strongest oxidising agent in the table.

2. (a) Use the electrochemical series in the SQA data booklet to predict whether the following reactions will take place:

    (i) $Br_2(aq) + 2I^-(aq) \rightarrow 2Br^-(aq) + I_2(aq)$

    (ii) $2Ag^+(aq) + Cu(s) \rightarrow 2Ag(s) + Cu^{2+}(aq)$

    (iii) $MnO_4^-(aq) + 2Cl^-(aq) \rightarrow Mn^{2+}(aq) + Cl_2(aq)$

    (iv) $F_2(g) + Cr_2O_7^{2-}(aq) \rightarrow 2Cr^{3+}(aq) + 2F^-(aq)$

    (b) For the reactions in (a) which do take place, use the electrochemical series to write oxidation and reduction ion–electron equations.

    (c) Combine the ion–electron equations in (b) to form redox equations.

    (d) Identify the oxidising and reducing agents in each reaction.

Learning checklist

Periodicity

In this section you have learned:

- Elements are arranged in the periodic table in order of increasing atomic number.
- Groups are vertical columns in the periodic table containing elements with similar chemical properties because they have the same number of electrons in the outer shell.
- Periods are rows of elements arranged in order of increasing atomic number and show a change from metallic to non-metallic character.
- The first 20 elements in the periodic table are categorised according to their bonding and structure:
  - metallic (Li, Be, Na, Mg, Al, K, Ca)
  - monatomic (He, Ne, Ar)
  - covalent molecular (H_2, N_2, O_2, F_2, Cl_2, P_4, S_8 and C (fullerenes))
  - covalent network (B, C (diamond and graphite), Si)

Metals
- Atoms are held together by an electrostatic attraction between positive nuclei and delocalised electrons.

Non-metals
Monatomic
- The noble gases are monatomic elements with weak London dispersion forces between the atoms.
- London dispersion forces are weak forces of attraction between atoms and molecules when temporary dipoles are formed within atoms or molecules.

Covalent molecular
- Hydrogen, nitrogen, oxygen and the halogens exist as individual diatomic molecules, with London dispersion forces between the molecules (intermolecular), and strong covalent bonds between the atoms in a molecule.
- Sulfur and phosphorus are small individual molecules with strong London dispersion forces between molecules, so are solids at room temperature.
- Carbon can exist as large individual covalent molecules (fullerenes), which have molecules with 60 carbon atoms or more.
- Fullerene molecules can be ball- or tube-shaped, and have relatively high melting (sublimation) points because of the large London dispersion forces between molecules.

Covalent network
- Carbon can exist as large covalent networks – for example, diamond and graphite.
- The carbon atoms in diamond are bonded to four other carbons in a large, strong three-dimensional network. This makes it very hard.
- The network structure of diamond results in it having a very high melting point.
- Diamond is a non-conductor of electricity because it has no delocalised electrons.

- Graphite forms a network in which each carbon is only bonded to three other carbons, which results in graphite having delocalised electrons. It therefore conducts electricity.
- The carbon atoms in graphite form hexagonal plates which are held together by London dispersion forces.
- The layers in graphite can be easily separated, which results in graphite not being as hard as diamond.
- Boron and silicon exist as covalent networks, and have properties associated with covalent networks, e.g. very high melting and boiling points.

Trends in the periodic table

- Patterns in changes of covalent radii, ionisation energy and electronegativity exist when going down a group or across a period in the periodic table.
- The covalent radius is a measure of the size of an atom.
- The covalent radius increases down a group as the number of occupied electron shells increases and screens the outer electrons from the pull of the nucleus.
- The covalent radius decreases going across a group as there is no increased screening effect. The electrons are added to the same electron shell.
- First ionisation energy is the energy required to remove one mole of electrons from one mole of gaseous atoms.
- First ionisation energy decreases down a group as the outer electrons get further from the nucleus and are screened from the pull of the nucleus by the shells of the inner electrons.
- First ionisation energy generally increases across a period as the outer electrons are held more tightly by the nucleus as electrons are added to the same energy level and the charge on the nucleus increases.
- Electronegativity is a measure of the attraction an atom has for the electrons of the bond.
- Electronegativity decreases down a group. Although the nuclear charge increases, the atoms get bigger and the screening effect of the inner shells of electrons increases so the attraction of the nucleus for bonding electrons decreases.
- Electronegativity increases across a period as the atoms get smaller because the nuclear charge increases, and the attraction of the nucleus for bonding electrons increases. There is no screening effect as the electrons are always added to the same shell.

Structure and bonding

In this section you have learned:
- In a covalent bond, atoms share pairs of electrons.
- The covalent bond is a result of two positive nuclei being held together by their common attraction for the shared pair of electrons.
- In pure covalent bonding, the shared pair of electrons is shared equally by the atoms in the molecule.
- In polar covalent bonding there is unequal sharing of the bonded electrons, which results in one atom having a slightly negative charge (δ^-), and the other having a slightly positive charge (δ^+). This creates a permanent dipole.

- Electronegativity is a numerical measurement on a scale of 0–4 (low to high) used to assess an element's ability to attract bonding electrons.
- The difference in electronegativity between the atoms in a compound gives an indication of the type of bonding present.
- The type of bonding changes gradually as the difference in electronegativity between atoms increases – this is known as the bonding continuum.
- The bonding continuum has ionic bonding at one end, and pure covalent bonding at the other. There is polar covalent bonding between the two extremes.
- Compounds formed between metals and non-metals are often, but not always, ionic – physical properties have to be considered when deciding bonding and structure.
- Intermolecular forces act between molecules and are known as van der Waals forces.
- London dispersion forces and permanent dipole–permanent dipole interactions including hydrogen bonding are van der Waals forces.
- London dispersion forces are the weakest attractions between temporary dipoles in molecules, and are significant between non-polar molecules. The more electrons in the molecule the stronger the force.
- Permanent dipole–permanent dipole interactions are additional attractions between polar molecules which have permanent dipoles which are stronger than London dispersion forces for molecules with similar numbers of electrons.
- A molecule will only be polar if one side of the molecule is slightly negative (δ^-) and the other slightly positive (δ^+).
- The melting and boiling points of polar substances are higher than the melting and boiling points of non-polar molecules with similar numbers of electrons.
- Hydrogen bonds form between highly polar molecules which have hydrogen bonded to the greatly electronegative elements fluorine, oxygen or nitrogen.
- Hydrogen bonding gives compounds unusually high melting and boiling points. This is because they are the strongest van der Waals force, and so need more energy to separate the molecules, e.g. water.
- When water is cooled to 4°C or below, it expands and decreases in density. This is due to the water molecules forming a more open structure, with increased hydrogen bonding.
- Compounds with molecules which have hydrogen bonding between them are more viscous than compounds with molecules which have other intermolecular forces.
- The polar nature of water makes it a good solvent for ionic compounds and polar covalent molecular compounds.
- Non-polar solvents can dissolve non-polar substances.
- The molecules of polar covalent liquids which are miscible with water form hydrogen bonds with water molecules.

Oxidising and reducing agents

In this section you have learned:

- Reduction is gain of electrons by a reactant.
- Oxidation is loss of electrons by a reactant.
- In a redox reaction reduction and oxidation take place at the same time.
- An oxidising agent is a substance which accepts electrons.
- A reducing agent is a substance which donates electrons.
- Oxidising agents are reduced.
- Reducing agents are oxidised.
- Elements can act as reducing and oxidising agents.
- Elements with low electronegativity values, like the group 1 metals, form ions by losing electrons and are strong reducing agents.
- Elements with high electronegativity values, like the group 7 elements, form ions by gaining electrons and are strong oxidising agents.
- How to write reduction and oxidation ion–electron equations involving elements.
- Compounds, group ions and molecules can act as oxidising and reducing agents.
- How to write reduction and oxidation ion–electron equations involving compounds, group ions and molecules.
- Given a group ion, work out the balanced ion–electron equation.
- How to balance reduction and oxidation ion–electron equations and combine them to form the redox equation.
- How to recognise oxidising and reducing agents in a redox equation.
- Carbon monoxide acts as a reducing agent.
- Hydrogen peroxide, acidified permanganate and acidified dichromate solutions are strong oxidising agents.
- The oxidising property of hydrogen peroxide makes it useful as a bleaching agent, to remove colour from materials.
- The oxidising property of the permanganate ion makes it effective in killing fungi and bacteria, and can also deactivate viruses.
- The electrochemical series lists substances in order of how well they act as reducing/oxidising agents.
- Strong reducing agents are found at the top-right of the electrochemical series.
- Strong oxidising agents are found at the bottom-left of the electrochemical series.
- Ion–electron equations in the electrochemical series are written as reductions, but can be reversed to obtain the oxidation equation.

Alcohols 1

Systematically naming alcohols

Alcohols have the hydroxyl functional group −OH. **Straight-chain** alcohols take their name from the corresponding alkane. The -e is dropped and replaced by -ol. The carbon atoms are numbered so that the −OH group has the lowest number.

Example:

$$H - \overset{\displaystyle H}{\underset{\displaystyle H}{C^4}} - \overset{\displaystyle H}{\underset{\displaystyle H}{C^3}} - \overset{\displaystyle H}{\underset{\displaystyle O}{C^2}} - \overset{\displaystyle H}{\underset{\displaystyle H}{C^1}} - H$$

Molecular formula: $C_4H_{10}O$

butan-2-ol

Branched-chain alcohols:

1. Name the longest carbon chain containing the hydroxyl group.
2. Number the chain from the end that the hydroxyl group is nearer to and identify the position of the hydroxyl group.

    Use prefixes if there is more than one side chain of the same type (e.g. di- is used if there are two of the same type, tri- if there are three, etc.).
3. Name the branches (side chains), e.g. CH_3 -methyl; C_2H_5 -ethyl, etc. Branches are ordered alphabetically in the name.
4. Indicate the position of the branches on the main chain.

Example:

Structural and molecular formulae from systematic names

Straight-chain alcohols:

Example:

hexan-3-ol

Structural formula

$C_6H_{12}O$

Molecular formula

Branched-chain alcohols:

1. Identify the number of carbon atoms in the longest straight chain containing the hydroxyl group.
2. Identify the position of the hydroxyl group.
3. Identify the branches and the numbers of the carbon atoms to which they are attached.

Example: Draw the structural formula for **2-ethyl-3-methylpentan-1-ol**.

1. Longest straight chain has 5 carbons.

| 2 – ethyl – 3 – methyl | pentan – 1 – ol |

3. C_2H_5 on carbon 2. CH_3 on carbon 3.

2. Hydroxyl on carbon 1.

Quick Test 10

1. Write the systematic name for the structure shown:

2. Draw the structural formula for 4-methylhexan-3-ol.

Alcohols 2

Classification of alcohols

Alcohols can be classified as primary, secondary and tertiary.

In **primary alcohols**, the carbon atom with the hydroxyl group is attached to **one** other carbon atom, e.g. propan-1-ol:

In **secondary alcohols**, the carbon atom with the hydroxyl group is attached to **two** other carbon atoms, e.g. propan-2-ol:

In **tertiary alcohols**, the carbon atom with the hydroxyl group is attached to **three** other carbon atoms, e.g. 2-methylpropan-2-ol:

TOP TIP

It is important to be able to classify alcohols in order to predict whether they will react. Although you don't need to be able to name complex alcohols, you should be able to classify them from their structural formula.

Diols and triols

Alcohols with **two hydroxyl groups** are referred to as **diols**.

The simplest diol is ethane-1,2-diol:

Alcohols with **three hydroxyl groups** are referred to as **triols**.

Glycerol is an example of a triol. Its systematic name is propane-1,2,3-triol. Glycerol is the alcohol part of fats and oils.

Diols and triols have high boiling points due to strong **hydrogen bonding** between molecules.

TOP TIP

The more hydroxyl groups an alcohol has, the stronger the hydrogen bonding. This means more energy is needed to separate the molecules, so the boiling point is higher.

Boiling points of alcohols

The bar chart shows the boiling points of alcohols with up to four carbon atoms. They are:

CH_3OH CH_3CH_2OH $CH_3CH_2CH_2OH$ $CH_3CH_2CH_2CH_2OH$
methanol   ethanol   propan-1-ol   butan-1-ol

They are compared with the equivalent alkanes (methane to butane) with the same number of carbon atoms.

Notice that the boiling point of an alcohol is always much higher than that of the alkane with the same number of carbon atoms.

The patterns in the boiling point reflect the patterns in intermolecular attractions. Alcohol molecules

have the polar −OH group, which results in hydrogen bonding between the molecules. Hydrogen bonds are stronger than the London dispersion forces which exist between the alkane molecules. This means it requires more energy to separate alcohol molecules from each other, and so their boiling points are higher.

Solubility of alcohols in water

Small alcohol molecules such as methanol and ethanol are very soluble and mix completely with water. The presence of the −OH group in both the alcohol and water molecules results in strong hydrogen bonding between the molecules.

In **large** alcohol molecules such as octan-1-ol the London dispersion forces between the hydrocarbon parts of the alcohol molecules are stronger than the hydrogen bonding, which makes it more difficult for large alcohol molecules to dissolve.

Quick Test 11

1. Write the systematic name for the alcohol shown and state its classification:

```
              H
              |
        H — C — H
        H   |   H   H   H
        |   |   |   |   |
H — O — C — C — C — C — C — H
        |   |   |   |   |
        H   |   H   H   H
        H — C — H
              |
              H
```

2. Draw the structural formula for 2-methylbutan-2-ol and state its classification.

3. Ethanol (b.p.: 78°C) and fluoroethane (b.p.: −37°C) have the same number of electrons in a molecule. Explain then why their boiling points are so different.

Carboxylic acids

Systematically naming carboxylic acids

Carboxylic acids have the carboxyl functional group −COOH at the end of the structure. **Straight-chain** carboxylic acids take their name from the corresponding alkane. The -e is dropped and replaced by -oic.

Branched carboxylic acids are named following the steps below:

1. Name the longest hydrocarbon chain containing the carboxyl group.

2. Name the branches, e.g. CH_3 -methyl; C_2H_5 -ethyl, etc. Branches are ordered alphabetically.

   Use prefixes if there is more than one side chain of the same type (e.g. di- is used if there are two of the same type, tri- if there are three, etc.)

3. Indicate the position of the branches on the main chain, numbering from the carboxyl group as carbon 1.

Example:

3. Branches on 2nd and 4th carbon		1. Longest straight chain has five carbons
2, 4	– dimethyl	pentanoic acid

2. Two methyl groups

Structural and molecular formulae from the systematic name

1. Identify the number of carbon atoms in the longest straight chain containing the carboxyl group.

2. Identify the branches and the numbers of the carbon atoms to which they are attached.

Example: The structural formula for 3-ethyl-2-methylhexanoic acid.

1. Longest straight chain has six carbons

3-ethyl-2-methyl	hexanoic acid

2. One C_2H_5 on carbon 3, one CH_3 on carbon 2

Molecular formula: $C_9H_{18}O_2$

Reacting carboxylic acids

Neutralisation

Carboxylic acids neutralise bases to form salts. The salt produced depends on the base reacted. The name of the salt always ends in -oate.

Examples:

1. sodium hydroxide + ethanoic acid → sodium ethanoate + water

$\quad$ NaOH $\quad$ + $\quad$ CH_3COOH $\quad$ → $\quad$ CH_3COONa $\quad$ + $\quad$ H_2O

2. potassium oxide + methanoic acid → potassium methanoate + water

$\quad$ K_2O $\quad$ + $\quad$ 2HCOOH $\quad$ → $\quad$ 2HCOOK $\quad$ + $\quad$ H_2O

3. calcium carbonate + propanoic acid → calcium propanoate + water + carbon dioxide

$\quad$ $CaCO_3$ $\quad$ + $\quad$ $2C_2H_5COOH$ → $2(C_2H_5COO)Ca$ + H_2O + CO_2

TOP TIP

Carboxylic acids show typical acid properties, and undergo neutralisation like common lab acids, such as hydrochloric acid.

Quick Test 12

1. State the systematic name for the carboxylic acid shown:

2. Draw the structural formula for 4-ethyl-3-methylheptanoic acid.

3. (a) Write a formula equation for propanoic acid reacting with magnesium carbonate.

   (b) Name the salt formed in part (a).

Esters, fats and oils 1

Making and using esters

Esters are formed by the **condensation** reaction between a carboxylic acid and an alcohol. Water is also produced. Concentrated sulfuric acid acts as a catalyst.

Many fruits get their distinctive flavour from esters. Artificial esters are widely used in the confectionary industry as flavouring for sweets. Some are used in perfumes because of their strong, pleasant smell. Others, like ethyl ethanoate, are used as solvents for products such as nail varnish which do not dissolve in water.

Naming esters

The first part of the name is derived from the alcohol and ends in **-yl**; the second part comes from the acid and ends in **-oate**.

TOP TIP

Although the first part of the name comes from the alcohol, the acid part of the ester is usually drawn on the left. Notice the way the structure of the alcohol is drawn to show how the hydroxyl group reacts with the carboxyl group.

Example

methanoic acid + ethanol ⇌ eth**yl** methan**oate** + water

Note: (1) is known as the **ester link**.

(2) The ester link is formed when the carboxyl group of the acid reacts with the hydroxyl group of the alcohol.

(3) **Water** is formed during the reaction.

(4) The ⇌ symbol indicates the reaction is reversible.

TOP TIP

Given the names of the parent carboxylic acid and alcohol or their structural formulae, you should be able to **name** the ester formed when they react.

TOP TIP

Given the names of the parent carboxylic acid and alcohol or the names of esters, you should be able to **draw** the structural formulae for esters.

Breaking esters

The formation of esters is reversible, so esters can be broken down into their parent acid and alcohol by reacting with water – this is known as **hydrolysis**. This requires the ester to be heated with a dilute acid or alkali to speed up the process.

When a dilute acid is used, the parent carboxylic acid and parent alcohol are obtained. When ethyl propanoate is hydrolysed using dilute acid, propanoic acid and ethanol are obtained.

> **TOP TIP**
>
> Given the name or the structural formula of an ester, the hydrolysis products can be named and their structural formulae drawn.

H   H   O ┊   H   H   H   H   O   H   H
│   │   ‖ ┊   │   │   O   │   │   ‖   │   │
H—C—C—C┊O—C—C—H   +   ⇌   H—C—C—C—O—H + H—O—C—C—H
│   │   ┊   │   │   H   H   │   │   │   │
H   H   ┊   H   H   H   H   H   H

ethyl propanoate   water   propanoic acid   ethanol

The molecule always splits at the ester link, as shown by the dotted line.

Quick Test 13

1. (a) Name the esters formed when the following carboxylic acids and alcohols react:

    (i) methanoic acid and propan-1-ol

    (ii)

    H   H   H   O   H   H
    │   │   │   ‖   │   │
    H—C—C—C—C—O—H   +   H—O—C—C—H
    │   │   │   │   │
    H   H   H   H   H

    (b) Draw the structural formulae for the esters formed.

2. Name the products formed when the following esters are hydrolysed under acid conditions, and draw their structural formulae.

    (a) ethyl ethanoate

    (b)

Esters, fats and oils 2

TOP TIP

Hydrolysis of a fat or oil will always give one mole of glycerol molecules to three moles of fatty acid molecules. The three fatty acids in a fat or oil molecule may be the same or different.

Edible fats and oils

Edible **fats and oils** are naturally occurring esters which come from animals (e.g. butter and fish oil) and plants (e.g. olive oil). They are a concentrated source of energy, and are essential for the storage and transport of fat-soluble vitamins in the body. Fats and oils are formed by a condensation reaction between long-chain carboxylic acids, often called **fatty acids**, and **glycerol** (propane-1,2,3-triol).

glycerol (propane-1,2,3-triol)   stearic acid (octadecanoic acid), a fatty acid

The hydrocarbon chain can be represented as a serrated line, or by the letter R, in order to simplify the structure of a fatty acid.

The hydrocarbon tail can be saturated or partially unsaturated, giving rise to a variety of fatty acids. The different hydrocarbon tails can be represented as R^1, R^2, R^3 and so forth.

Glycerol has three hydroxyl groups in each molecule and so reacts with three fatty acid molecules. This results in each fatty acid molecule forming an ester link with the glycerol molecule. This is why fats and oils are sometimes called triglycerides. One of the ester links in a triglyceride molecule is shown within the dotted area in the diagram on the right.

If the fatty acid chains are mostly **saturated**, the substance will likely be solid at room temperature and be called a **fat**. The greater the proportion of **unsaturated** fatty acid chains, the more likely the triglyceride is to be liquid at room temperature. In this case, it is called an **oil**.

A simplified triglyceride molecule, highlighting one of the ester links in the molecule.

The structure of fats and oils

In **fats**, the shape of the molecules allows them to pack closer together with stronger van der Waals forces between them than is the case with oils. This means fats need more energy to separate the molecules, and are therefore solids at room temperature.

In **oils**, the presence of double bonds on the fatty acid parts of the molecules causes the hydrocarbon chains of the fatty acids to be more kinked. This means the molecules are unable to pack as closely together. This indicates that the van der Waals forces are weaker, and so it takes less energy to separate them. Triglycerides with double bonds have a lower melting point, and tend to be liquids (oils).

This is shown in the simplified diagrams below.

A simplified 'tuning fork' representation of fat molecules showing the van der Waals attractions between molecules.

The double bonds in oil molecules 'kink' the tail of the molecule, which means they don't pack as easily as fat molecules.

The fats in butter are mostly saturated while oils are mostly unsaturated.

The amount of unsaturation in a fat or oil can be compared by adding bromine solution. The greater the unsaturation the more bromine solution is decolourised. The bromine molecules add across the C=C double bonds in an addition reaction.

TOP TIP

Fat and oil molecules have very complicated structures. Simplified structures are used to help explain how they are formed and to explain their properties. Fats and oils are esters – look out for the ester link in their structures.

Quick Test 14

1. Explain why a fat molecule has three ester links.

2. Suggest a chemical test that you could use to show that oil molecules are unsaturated.

3. (a) Explain why fats are solid at room temperature while oils are liquid.

   (b) Suggest why some oils go solid if placed in the fridge.

Soaps, detergents and emulsions 1

Soap

Fats and oils are esters. When they are hydrolysed using alkali, salts of the long-chain fatty acids are formed. These are **soaps**. Glycerol is also formed and can be used in the food and pharmaceutical industries.

$$
\begin{array}{c}
\text{H}-\text{C}-\text{O}-\text{C}-(\text{CH}_2)_{16}\text{CH}_3 \\
\text{H}-\text{C}-\text{O}-\text{C}-(\text{CH}_2)_{16}\text{CH}_3 + 3\text{Na}^+\text{OH}^- \longrightarrow \\
\text{H}-\text{C}-\text{O}-\text{C}-(\text{CH}_2)_{16}\text{CH}_3
\end{array}
$$

fat (triglyceride)

$$
\begin{array}{c}
\text{H}-\text{C}-\text{O}-\text{H} \\
\text{H}-\text{C}-\text{O}-\text{H} \\
\text{H}-\text{C}-\text{O}-\text{H}
\end{array}
+ 3\text{Na}^+ \ ^-\text{O}-\text{C}-(\text{CH}_2)_{16}\text{CH}_3
$$

glycerol   sodium stearate (soap)

Structure of soap 'molecules'

A soap molecule has a long covalent hydrocarbon part, often referred to as the tail, and an ionic part, often referred to as the head.

hydrophobic but oil soluble · hydrophilic or water soluble

covalent hydrocarbon tail · ionic head

TOP TIP

Although often referred to as a 'molecule', soap is a salt and has ionic and covalent parts.

The tail, being covalent and non-polar, will be insoluble in water. It is termed **hydrophobic**, which means '**water-hating**'. It is, however, soluble in covalent substances such as grease and oil.

The negatively charged head of the soap ion is termed **hydrophilic**, which means '**water-loving**'.

Cleansing action of soap

When soap is used to clean oil or grease from a surface, the hydrophobic tails of the soap ions bury into the oil and grease. Agitation causes small grease droplets (micelles) to form in the water. The negative charges on the heads repel each other and prevent the globules of oil from recombining. This allows the oil or grease to be washed off the surface.

(a) soap dissolves in water, forming soap ions

(b) tails of soap ions bury into grease, leaving heads in water

(c) agitation begins to separate grease from surface

(d) process continues, forming grease globules (micelles) in the water

(e) micelles are prevented from recombining by negative charges on heads of soap ions in the water

soap ions

grease

surface

clean surface

One problem with soap is that it does not lather well in hard-water areas. Hard water contains calcium and magnesium ions. Insoluble salts like calcium stearate, known as scum, form. Detergents have been developed which do not form a scum.

Detergents

Detergents are cleaning agents which work in a similar way to soaps, but have the advantage of not forming insoluble salts in hard water. This means they can form a lather. Alkylbenzenesulfonates such as sodium dodecylbenzenesulfonate are detergents. They have a similar structure to soaps, in that they have a hydrophobic hydrocarbon tail and a hydrophilic ionic head. As a result, they clean in the same way as soaps.

The manufacture of detergents as cleansing agents is lucrative business all over the world.

sodium dodecylbenzenesulfonate: $CH_3(CH_2)_{11}C_6H_4$ $SO_3^- Na^+$

hydrocarbon tail   ionic head

The most common way of making dodecylbenzenesulfonate is by reacting benzene, C_6H_6, (from the oil industry) with dodecene ($C_{12}H_{24}$) and sulfur trioxide to give the sulfonic acid. The sulfonic acid is then neutralised with sodium hydroxide.

Quick Test 15

1. Explain why soap molecules are also called salts.
2. Describe the cleansing action of a soap molecule.
3. Explain why detergents can form a lather in hard-water areas.

Soaps, detergents and emulsions 2

Emulsions

An **emulsion** is a mixture of two or more liquids that are normally immiscible. The emulsion contains small droplets of one liquid dispersed in another, with the aid of an **emulsifier**. Emulsifiers allow normally immiscible liquids to mix and stop them separating.

Emulsions in food are mixtures of a fat/oil and water. Milk and mayonnaise are examples of emulsions. The natural emulsifier in milk is a protein called casein.

Emulsifiers are soap-like molecules that can be made by reacting edible oils with glycerol. One or two fatty acid groups are attached to the glycerol backbone, rather than the three in fats/oils (see 'Edible fats and oils' page 44). This results in the emulsifier having molecules with a hydrophobic part (the fatty acid 'tail') and a hydrophilic part – one or two hydroxyl groups or other water-soluble parts.

Monoglyceride

Diglyceride

In the emulsion, the hydrophobic part of the emulsifier dissolves in the fat/oil, and the hydrophilic part dissolves in the water. This holds the mixture together.

The inclusion of food additives is indicated on food labels by E numbers. The emulsifier known as E471 is the most commonly used emulsifier in the food industry. It contains a mixture of mono- and di-glycerides. Lecithin, found naturally in egg yolks, acts as the emulsifier in mayonnaise. The table on the next page gives some examples of foods that contain common emulsifiers.

Emulsifier	E number	Food product
lecithin	322	chocolate, margarine, chewing gum
mono- and di-glycerides	471	ice cream, bread, sausages

Adding mono- and di-glycerides to breads and cakes improves the texture and volume of the products. They keep cakes and bread soft, improving shelf life.

Emulsifiers help maintain quality and freshness. In low-fat spreads, emulsifiers help prevent the growth of moulds, which would happen if the oil and fat separated.

Processed meats like salami contain mono- and di-glycerides as emulsifiers to ensure the even distribution of fat.

TOP TIP

The structures of emulsifiers are complicated. You are not expected to memorise them, but you should be able to recognise their structure. It is similar to fats and oils, but at least one of the fatty acids in the structure has been replaced by a hydrophilic group, such as –OH.

BERTOLLI LIGHT SPREAD MADE ● W

38% VEGETABLE FAT SPREAD WITH 16% OLIVE OIL

Ingredients: Water, Olive Oil composed of Refined Olive Oils and Virgin Olive Oils (16%), Vegetable Oil, Modified Starch, Salt (0.8%), Buttermilk, Emulsifiers (Mono-and Di-glycerides of Fatty Acids, Sunflower Lecithin), Preservative (Potassium Sorbate), Citric Acid, Flavourings, Colour (Beta-Carotene), Vitamin A and D.

Vegetable fat spreads contain emulsifiers.

Quick Test 16

1. Polysorbate 80 is used as an emulsifier in ice cream. Describe the properties that polysorbate 80 is likely to have that make it useful as an emulsifier.

Proteins

Proteins

Proteins are needed in our diet for growth and repair of body tissue, for example hair, nails and muscle. Proteins are also responsible for the maintenance and regulation of life processes.

Amino acids

Proteins are natural condensation polymers made up of **amino acids**. Each amino acid has two functional groups, an **amino group**, **$-NH_2$**, and a **carboxyl group**, **$-COOH$**.

The structure of an amino acid can be represented as:

TOP TIP

If you are asked to show how amino acids join, disregard the R groups and focus on where the carboxylic acid and amino acid groups are.

R varies and can be, for example, H, CH_3, etc. and can also contain S, N and O.

There are 20 amino acids needed by the body to make proteins. These amino acids combine in varying amounts and in different sequences. The body cannot make all the amino acids needed, and so relies on food for these **essential amino acids**.

When two amino acids join, a water molecule is also produced. The diagram below shows three amino acids joining to form part of a protein structure:

glycine   alanine   serine

TOP TIP

A protein can be identified by the presence of the peptide link in the structure:

part of a protein molecule

The new link formed between the amino acids is known as the **peptide** (or amide) **link**.

Enzymes

Enzymes are responsible for the many chemical reactions which take place in our bodies. Most enzymes are proteins. Enzymes are described as **biological catalysts** because they speed up biochemical reactions, as well as the digestion of dietary protein.

When dietary protein is **hydrolysed** in the body amino acids are formed. The hydrolysis takes place at the peptide link.

TOP TIP

Given part of a protein structure, you should be able to draw the amino acids obtained by hydrolysis of the protein. Hydrolysis always takes place at the peptide link – H always adds to the amino acid part and OH to the carboxylic acid part.

Denaturing protein

Proteins are long chain molecules that can be twisted to form spirals and folded into sheets. The chains are held in these forms by intermolecular bonding within the molecule. When heated, these forces of attraction are broken and the protein is **denatured** – it loses its shape.

The white of an egg (albumen) is a globular protein – the chains are clumped together in small balls. When heated, the strands unwind as intermolecular bonds are broken. New bonds form between protein strands, resulting in the familiar white colour and texture of cooked egg.

Quick Test 17

1. (a) (i) Draw part of the protein structure formed when the three amino acids shown below join.

glycine · phenylalanine · alanine

   (ii) Circle the peptide links in the structure.

2. Draw the structural formulae for the amino acids formed when the protein structure shown below is hydrolysed.

Oxidation of food 1

Aldehydes and ketones

The flavour in foods is the result of a complex mixture of chemicals, including **aldehydes** and **ketones**, which both contain the **carbonyl group**:

$$\begin{array}{c} O \\ \| \\ C \\ / \ \backslash \end{array}$$

TOP TIP

The functional groups in aldehydes are always written as –CHO to distinguish them from alcohols, –COH.

Aldehydes always have the carbonyl functional group at the end of the structure and at least one hydrogen attached to the carbonyl group. Ketones have no hydrogens attached to the carbonyl group – there are always two carbons attached. Aldehydes have the name ending -al. Ketones have the name ending -one. Both take the first part of their name from the corresponding alkane. See the table below for examples of a straight-chain aldehyde and ketone.

TOP TIP

Aldehydes and ketones from C_3 upwards, exhibit isomerism (see page 58).

Name	Structural formula	Shortened structural formula	Molecular formula
propan**al**	H, H, O structure: H—C—C—C—H	CH_3CH_2CHO	C_3H_6O
propan**one**	H, O, H structure: H—C—C—C—H	CH_3COCH_3	C_3H_6O

TOP TIP

Although you will not be asked to name complex aldehydes and ketones, you may be given a name or structural formula and asked to identify it as either an aldehyde or ketone.

Boiling points

Carbonyl compounds are polar. They contain a dipole along the carbon–oxygen double bond. This creates permanent dipole–permanent dipole attractions between molecules. These forces of attraction result in aldehydes and ketones having boiling points that are higher than their equivalent alkane (due to weaker London dispersion forces) but lower than their corresponding alcohol (due to stronger hydrogen bonding). Small aldehydes and ketones are very volatile, so even gently warming them causes them to emit odours often associated with cooking certain foods.

Solubility

Carbonyl compounds can form hydrogen bonds with water molecules, meaning that lower molecular mass aldehydes and ketones are soluble (miscible) in water.

Some foods, like asparagus, have water-soluble flavour molecules so they lose flavour if boiled. Others, like broccoli, have flavour molecules which are more soluble in oil so they don't lose flavour by cooking them in water.

Quick Test 18

1. The carvone molecule shown is what gives spearmint its smell and flavour. It is used in the manufacture of some spearmint gums.

   (a) Circle the carbonyl group in the structure.

   (b) State whether carvone is an aldehyde or ketone and explain your answer.

   (c) What does the use of carvone suggest about its volatility?

2. Draw the structural formulae of the straight-chain aldehyde and ketone with five carbon atoms and write their molecular formulae.

Oxidation of food 2

Systematically naming branched-chain aldehydes and drawing structural formulae

Using the systematic naming rules, given the structural formula:

1. Name the longest hydrocarbon chain.

2. Name the branches (side chains), e.g. CH_3 -methyl; C_2H_5 -ethyl; etc.

   Prefixes are used if there is more than one side chain of the same type (e.g. di- is used if there are two of the same type, tri- if there are three, and so forth).

3. Indicate the position of the branches on the main chain, numbering from the carbonyl group as carbon 1.

   Example:

TOP TIP

Given the structural formulae of straight-chain or branched-chain aldehydes and ketones, you should be able to name those with up to eight carbons. Given the names of straight-chain or branched-chain aldehydes and ketones, you should be able to draw their structural formulae and write their molecular formulae.

Given the systematic name, you can draw the structural formulae for branched-chain aldehydes:

1. Identify the number of carbon atoms in the longest straight-chain.

2. Identify the branches and the numbers of the carbon atoms to which they are attached.

Naming ketones from structural formulae

Straight-chain ketones are named in a similar way to alcohols, except their suffix is -one.

Example:

TOP TIP

Pentan-2-one and pentan-3-one are isomers. In ketone isomers, the position of the carbonyl group can move, and there is the possibility of branches. In aldehyde isomers the position of the carbonyl must always be on the end carbon, however the branches can vary.

pentan-2-one   pentan-3-one

Systematically naming branched-chain ketones and drawing structural formulae

Use the systematic naming rules, given the structural formula:

1. Name the longest carbon chain containing the carbonyl group.
2. Number the chain from the end that the carbonyl group is nearer to, and identify the position of the carbonyl group.
3. Name the branches (side chains), e.g. CH_3 -methyl; C_2H_5 -ethyl; etc. **(**Prefixes are used if there is more than one side chain of the same type (e.g. di- is used if there are two of the same type, tri- if there are three, etc.)
4. Indicate the position of the branches on the main chain.

Example:

4. Branches on 3rd and 4th carbon   1. Six carbons

| 3 – | ethyl | – 4 – | methyl | hexan – 2 – one |

3. Two branches   2. Carbonyl on carbon 2

Given the systematic name, you can draw the structural formulae for branched-chain aldehydes.

1. Identify the number of carbon atoms in the longest straight chain containing the carbonyl group.
2. Identify the position of the carbonyl group.
3. Identify the branches and the numbers of the carbon atoms to which they are attached.

Quick Test 19

1. (a) Draw structural formulae for 3-methylpentanal and 4-methylpentan-2-one.

   (b) Write the molecular formula for both structures.

   (c) A student stated that the two compounds in (a) couldn't be isomers because they belong to different homologous series. Comment on this statement.

2. Write the systematic names for structures A and B.

A   B

Oxidation of food 3

Oxidation of alcohols

If a product molecule has a larger oxygen:hydrogen ratio than the reactant, then oxidation has taken place.

Primary alcohols can be oxidised to **aldehydes** then **carboxylic acids**.

Example:

	ethanol	ethanal	ethanoic acid
O:H ratio :	1:6	1:4	1:2
	(0·17)	(0·25)	(0·50)

Secondary alcohols are oxidised to **ketones**.

Example:

propan-2-ol → propanone

$$H-\overset{\overset{\displaystyle H}{|}}{\underset{\underset{\displaystyle H}{|}}{C}}-\overset{\overset{\displaystyle H}{|}}{\underset{\underset{\displaystyle OH}{|}}{C}}-\overset{\overset{\displaystyle H}{|}}{\underset{\underset{\displaystyle H}{|}}{C}}-H \rightarrow H-\overset{\overset{\displaystyle H}{|}}{\underset{\underset{\displaystyle H}{|}}{C}}-\overset{\overset{\displaystyle }{||}}{\underset{\underset{\displaystyle O}{}}{C}}-\overset{\overset{\displaystyle H}{|}}{\underset{\underset{\displaystyle H}{|}}{C}}-H$$

O:H ratio :	1:8	1:6
	(0·13)	(0·17)

TOP TIP

Confused about ratios? Think in fractions! Remember 1:6 (1/6 = 0·17)
1:4 (1/4 = 0·25)
0·17 < 0·25
So, going from 1:6 to 1:4 represents an increase in the oxygen to hydrogen ratio. Reduction is a **decrease** in the O:H ratio. **Tertiary** alcohols **cannot** be oxidised.

The oxidising agents are:

Hot copper(II) oxide (black) – the copper ions are reduced:
$Cu^{2+} + 2e^- \rightarrow Cu$ (brown)

Acidified dichromate – the dichromate ion (orange) is reduced to the chromium(III) ion (green): $Cr_2O_7^{2-}(aq) + 14H^+(aq) + 6e^- \rightarrow 2Cr^{3+}(aq) + 7H_2O(\ell)$

Oxidation of aldehydes

Although aldehydes and ketones both contain the carbonyl functional group, aldehydes can be **oxidised** whereas ketones cannot.

When an aldehyde is oxidised a carboxylic acid is formed. For example, ethanal would be oxidised to ethanoic acid.

$$CH_3CHO(\ell) + [O] \rightarrow CH_3COOH(\ell)$$

O:H ratio	1:4 (0·25)	2:4 (0·5)

An increase in the O:H ratio indicates oxidation has taken place.

Distinguishing aldehydes from ketones

The fact that aldehydes can be oxidised but ketones can't is useful for telling them apart. Three oxidising agents can be used to distinguish aldehydes and ketones: acidified potassium dichromate, Fehling's solution and Tollens' reagent. A few drops of the compound to be tested are added to the chosen reagent in a test tube and placed in a hot water bath. Each of the reagents gives a distinctive result with aldehydes only.

Acidified potassium dichromate

Orange dichromate ions are **reduced** to green chromium(III) ions.

$$Cr_2O_7^{2-}(aq) \ + \ 14H^+(aq) \ + \ 6e^- \ \rightarrow \ 2Cr^{3+}(aq) \ + \ 7H_2O(\ell)$$

orange   green

Fehling's solution

Fehling's solution is an alkaline solution containing copper(II) ions. The blue copper(II) ions are **reduced**, giving a precipitate of red/brown copper(I) oxide. The simplified equation is:

$$2Cu^{2+}(aq) \ + \ 2OH^-(aq) \ + \ 2e^- \ \rightarrow \ Cu_2O(s) \ + \ H_2O(\ell) \ + \ 2e^-$$

blue   red/brown

Tollens' reagent

Tollens' reagent is ammoniacal silver nitrate, and contains colourless silver(I) ions. Aldehydes **reduce** the silver ions to the metal and a very thin layer of silver metal is deposited on the test tube. The test is often referred to as the 'silver mirror test'.

$$Ag^+(aq) \ + \ e^- \ \rightarrow \ Ag(s)$$

colourless   silver mirror

Quick Test 20

1. (a) Compounds A, B and C were known to be either aldehydes or ketones. The table shows the results of chemical tests carried out on the compounds. Fill in the missing answers (i)–(v).

Compound	Reagent	Test result	Aldehyde/Ketone?
A	(i)	orange → (ii)	aldehyde
B	Tollens'	no change	(iii)
C	(iv)	blue → red/brown	(v)

    (b) Compounds B and C were found to have the molecular formula C_4H_8O. Draw the structural formulae for B and C and name the compounds.

    (c) Compound A is oxidised during the reaction. Name the type of compound formed when A is oxidised.

2. The conversion of ethanoic acid to ethanol is an example of reduction.
    Use oxygen:hydrogen ratios to explain this.

Oxidation of food 4 and isomerism

Antioxidants

Oxygen in the air can react with the chemicals in foods, causing them to spoil. Oils are particularly susceptible to oxidation. Many products (including free fatty acids) are formed, some of which have an unpleasant smell and taste. These fatty acids can be further oxidised at the double bonds, releasing volatile aldehydes which also smell. When an oil or fat is oxidised in this way, it is often said to be rancid.

To reduce the oxidation of chemicals in food, **antioxidants** are added to foodstuffs. If used properly, they can extend the shelf life of these products considerably.

Some antioxidants react with oxygen in preference to the foodstuff, and others prevent the formation of soapy-tasting peroxides.

A common antioxidant used in foodstuffs is ascorbic acid (vitamin C). The hydroxyl groups attached to the two carbons in the ring are oxidised to carbonyl groups.

| O:H ratio : | 6:8 (3:4 = 0·75) | 6:6 (3:3 = 1) |

The ion–electron equation and the oxygen:hydrogen ratio both indicate that the process is oxidation.

Isomerism

Isomers are molecules that have the same molecular formula, but have a different arrangement of the atoms in space.

Chain isomerism

In chain isomerism, the atoms are arranged in a completely different order, which results in branches.

Example 1: Aldehydes with the molecular formula $C_5H_{10}O$:

> **TOP TIP**
>
> Esters, aldehydes, ketones, alcohols and carboxylic acids can all exhibit some type of isomerism.

Straight chain   2-methylbutanal   3-methylbutanal

Branched chains

Example 2: Carboxylic acids with the molecular formula $C_5H_{10}O_2$:

2-methylbutanoic acid   3-methylbutanoic acid

Position isomerism

In position isomerism, the basic carbon skeleton remains unchanged, but functional groups can be moved around on that skeleton.

Example 3: Ketones with the molecular formula $C_7H_{14}O$:

4-methylhexan-2-one   4-methylhexan-3-one

> **TOP TIP**
>
> Aldehydes and carboxylic acids can't have positional isomers, because the functional group must always be on the end carbon.

Example 4: Alcohols with the molecular formula $C_6H_{14}O$:

3-methylpentan-1-ol   3-methylpentan-2-ol

> **TOP TIP**
>
> Ketones and alcohols can also have chain isomers, i.e. branches in different positions.

Functional group isomerism

Functional group isomers contain different functional groups – that is, they belong to different families of compounds (different homologous series).

Example 5: Propanoic acid and methyl ethanoate (molecular formula: $C_3H_6O_2$):

propanoic acid   methyl ethanoate

> **TOP TIP**
>
> If you are asked to draw the isomers from a given molecular formula, don't forget to think about all the possibilities. Can you branch the carbon chain? Can you move a functional group around on that chain? Is it possible to make more than one type of compound?

Quick Test 21

1. Draw aldehyde chain isomers with the molecular formula C_4H_8O and name them.

2. Draw aldehyde/ketone functional group isomers with the molecular formula C_3H_6O and name them.

Fragrances

Essential oils

Fragrances are pleasant, sweet-smelling liquids, derived from **essential oils** in plants. Essential oils get their name from the word 'essence' and are the concentrated extracts of the volatile non-water soluble aroma compounds found in plants. They are widely used in perfumes, cosmetic products, cleaning products, and even as flavourings in food.

Terpenes

TOP TIP

You don't need to memorise the names and structures of terpenes, but you should be able to recognise a terpene from a given structural formula.

Essential oils are composed mainly of a class of compounds known as **terpenes.**

Terpenes are molecules that can be viewed as being based on isoprene units, 2-methylbuta-1,3-diene, joined together.

Isoprene is a gaseous hydrocarbon which is naturally produced by different plants and emitted through their leaves into the atmosphere. Plants use isoprene to create terpenes by a complex biochemical process.

isoprene (2-methylbuta-1,3-diene)

The term **terpene** is often used to include terpene derivatives such as terpene alcohols, or aldehydes and ketones based on terpenes. The name ending normally indicates the functional group present. For example, -ene will indicate it is a hydrocarbon; -ol will indicate it contains a hydroxyl functional group, etc.

Geraniol can be extracted from the stems of the geranium plant.

myrcene

geraniol

Myrcene and geraniol are **linear** terpenes – they are open chains.

Limonene is an example of a cyclic terpene.

Terpenes are classified according to the number of isoprene units that are joined together. The main classes of terpene in the essential oil plants are shown in the following table.

limonene

Class of terpene	Number of isoprene units	Formula	Example
monoterpene	2	$C_{10}H_{16}$	myrcene
sesquiterpene	3	$C_{15}H_{24}$	humulene
diterpene	4	$C_{20}H_{32}$	neocembrene

Oxidation of terpenes

Terpenes can oxidise easily. Oxidation of terpenes in plants is often responsible for the distinctive aroma of spices. Peppermint oil, for example, contains the terpene menthol as well as its oxidation product menthone. Both contribute to the peppermint flavour of the oil.

menthol → oxidation → menthone

Quick Test 22

1. The structure of the terpene farnesol is shown below:

    (a) State which class of terpene farnesol belongs to.

    (b) Circle one isoprene unit in farnesol.

2. Limonene is a terpene found in orange juice which forms carvone if left exposed to the air:

    limonene   carvone

    (a) State the type of reaction undergone by limonene.

    (b) An alcohol called carveol is also formed. Draw a possible structural formula for carveol.

Skin care 1

The damaging effect of ultraviolet (UV) radiation on skin

Sunlight is composed of many types of light, including invisible **ultraviolet (UV) light**. UV is high-energy radiation which causes many chemical reactions in our skin, including the production of vitamin D, tanning, burning and ageing. To prevent sunburn, **sun blocks** have been developed. They contain compounds such as titanium dioxide which reflect the UV light and stop it reaching the skin. Sun screens contain chemicals which act as UV filters and reduce the amount of UV reaching the skin.

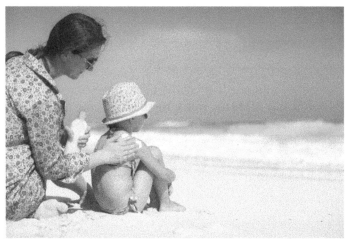

Sun creams contain sun block to reflect harmful UV rays.

Excessive exposure to the sun can cause you to look much older. The sun's rays change the skin's texture by weakening its elasticity. This causes the skin to sag and appear leathery.

Free radical reactions

Exposure to UV light can result in molecules gaining enough energy for chemical bonds to be broken. This is the process responsible for sunburn, and also contributes to the ageing of skin. When UV light breaks bonds **free radicals** are formed. Free radicals have unpaired electrons, and so are very reactive. Free radicals will react quickly with neighbouring atoms to form new bonds. This gives rise to a **free radical chain reaction**.

There are three stages in a free radical chain reaction: initiation, propagation and termination.

Initiation: The first step, where free radicals are formed when a molecule absorbs radiation.

Propagation: Steps in which free radicals react, forming further free radicals that can themselves react.

Termination: Steps in which free radicals combine, slowing the rate and stopping the reaction.

> **TOP TIP**
>
> Reactions which are initiated by light are known as photochemical reactions.

> **TOP TIP**
>
> Free radicals have no charge and are represented as $X\bullet$ (g).

Example

The reaction of chlorine with hydrogen

Hydrogen and chlorine do not react until a bright light is shone at them. When the light is shone at them the gases react explosively.

Initiation: The UV light splits the chlorine molecule into two chlorine free radicals:
$$Cl_2(g) \quad \rightarrow \quad 2Cl\bullet(g)$$

Propagation: The chlorine radicals react with hydrogen molecules:

$$Cl\bullet(g) \; + \; H_2(g) \quad \rightarrow \quad HCl(g) \; + \; H\bullet(g)$$

The hydrogen free radical formed can react with a chlorine molecule:

$$H\bullet(g) \; + \; Cl_2(g) \quad \rightarrow \quad HCl(g) \; + \; Cl\bullet(g)$$

Termination: The reaction continues until all the molecules have been used up and the remaining free radicals have combined together:

$$H\bullet(g) \; + \; Cl\bullet(g) \quad \rightarrow \quad HCl(g)$$

TOP TIP

The propagation part of the reaction must have at least two steps. The termination step in any free radical chain reaction occurs when any of the radicals combine and no new radicals are formed.

Quick Test 23

1. Chlorine-containing compounds which reach the upper atmosphere are known to produce radicals which are destroying the ozone (O_3) layer.

   The reactions listed below are known to take place, but not in the order shown:

   (i) $ClO\bullet + O\bullet \; \rightarrow \; Cl\bullet + O_2$

   (ii) $CF_3Cl \; \rightarrow \; CF_3\bullet + Cl\bullet$

   (iii) $CF_3\bullet + CF_3\bullet \; \rightarrow \; C_2F_6$

   (iv) $Cl\bullet + O_3 \; \rightarrow \; ClO\bullet + O_2$

   (a) State what kind of reaction is taking place overall.

   (b) Step (iv) is a propagation step. State what each of steps (i)–(iii) are.

   (c) Suggest where the energy to start the reaction comes from.

   (d) Suggest why the C–Cl bond breaks in preference to the C–F bond.

Skin care 2

Free radical scavengers

Our bodies produce chemicals which will react with free radicals that might otherwise cause damage to cells. These substances are known as **free radical scavengers**. Antioxidants are free radical scavengers. These substances work by reacting with and removing the free radicals, and stopping chain reactions which would otherwise damage the cells. The process doesn't completely prevent damage, and becomes less effective as we grow older.

Free radical scavengers in foods

Many foods contain natural antioxidants such as vitamins C and E. There is strong evidence to support the health benefits of a class of compounds called polyphenols, particularly in compounds known as flavonoids. The herbs parsley and thyme are good sources of the flavonoid luteolin.

Parsley   *Thyme*   **luteolin**

Fruits such as blueberries and raspberries are a source of antioxidants.

Antioxidants are also added to certain foods to help prevent the food from spoiling.

Free radical scavengers in cosmetics

Many creams contain compounds derived from vitamin C and vitamin E, which are powerful free radical scavengers. However, the effectiveness of compounds derived from them is disputed. Recent research has focused on polyphenols. They have been found to be able to pass into the epidermis and dermis, which demonstrates their potential as active ingredients in anti-ageing cosmetic products.

Free radical scavengers in plastics

Free radicals created in the atmosphere by UV radiation can cause plastics to degrade. Plastics such as polypropene and LDPE (low density polyethene) can discolour and crack. Oxygen reacts with the carbons in the polymer chains, forming carbonyl groups and weakening the plastics. Free radical scavengers are added to the plastics as UV stabilisers during the manufacturing process.

One common free radical scavenger added to plastics is benzophenone. It will react with reactive oxygen species, preventing damage to the polymer chains.

The durability of plastics used to make children's playground furniture is improved by incorporating free radical scavengers into them during the manufacturing process.

Benzophenone

Quick Test 24

1.   Explain the need for free radical scavengers.
2.   Give three examples of free radical scavengers and where they are used.

Learning checklist

Alcohols

In this section you have learned:

- Alcohols contain the hydroxyl functional group, −OH.
- When given the systematic name for a straight- and branched-chain alcohol with up to eight carbons in the main chain, a structural formula can be drawn and molecular formula written.
- When given the structure for a straight- or branched-chain alcohol with up to eight carbons in the main chain, it can be systematically named.
- Alcohols can be classified as primary, secondary or tertiary according to the number of carbon atoms that the carbon that is bonded to the hydroxyl group is attached to.
- Diols are alcohols with two hydroxyl groups and triols are alcohols with three hydroxyl groups.
- The ability to form hydrogen bonds affects properties of alcohols.
- Alcohols exhibit isomerism.

Carboxylic acids

In this section you have learned:

- Carboxylic acids contain the carboxyl group, −COOH.
- When given the systematic name for a straight- or branched-chain carboxylic acid with up to eight carbons in the main chain, a structural formula can be drawn and molecular formula written.
- When given the structure for a straight- or branched-chain carboxylic acid with up to eight carbons in the main chain, it can be systematically named.
- Carboxylic acids react with bases in neutralisation reactions to form salts.
- Carboxylic acids exhibit isomerism.

Esters, fats and oils

In this section you have learned:

- An ester can be identified from the presence of the ester group:

- The ester name is in the form -yl -oate, where the first part of the name is derived from the parent alcohol and the second part from the parent carboxylic acid.

- Structural formulae for esters can be drawn given the name of the parent alcohol and parent carboxylic acid or given the name of the ester.

- Esters can exhibit isomerism.

- Esters have characteristic smells and are used as flavourings.

- Esters are used as solvents for non-polar compounds.

- Esters can be made by reacting alcohols with carboxylic acids.

- Ester formation is an example of a condensation reaction.

- The ester link is formed when the hydroxyl group of the alcohol reacts with the carboxyl group of the acid, eliminating a small molecule of water in the process.

- Esters can be broken down (hydrolysed) into the parent alcohol and carboxylic acid.

- During hydrolysis a molecule breaks down into smaller molecules by reacting with water.

- The products of hydrolysis of an ester can be named, molecular formulae written and structural formulae drawn.

- Edible fats and oils are naturally occurring esters formed by the condensation of glycerol (propane-1,2,3-triol) with three long-chain carboxylic acid molecules known as fatty acids.

- Fatty acids can be saturated or unsaturated.

- The lower melting point of oils is related to the degree of unsaturation in the fatty acids.

- Molecules in oils cannot pack as closely as those in fats, leading to weaker intermolecular attractions and lower melting points.

- The more double bonds there are in the fatty acids in a fat or oil the more bromine solution it can decolourise.

- Fats and oils are an essential part of our diet, providing a concentrated energy source, and also transport fat-soluble vitamins in our bodies.

Soaps, detergents and emulsions

In this section you have learned:

- Hydrolysis of fats and oils in alkaline conditions produces soaps.
- Soap molecules have an ionic head and a hydrocarbon tail.
- The ionic head is hydrophilic (water loving) and dissolves well in water.
- The hydrocarbon tail is hydrophobic (water hating) and dissolves well in grease and oil.
- How to explain the cleaning action of soap.
- Hard water contains calcium and magnesium ions which form a scum with soap.
- Detergents were developed to combat hard water conditions.
- Detergents clean in the same way as soaps.
- Emulsions are formed when two normally immiscible liquids mix.
- Emulsifiers are compounds which allow two normally immiscible liquids to mix.
- Food emulsifiers are made by reacting edible oils with glycerol. Only one or two fatty acid groups are linked to each glycerol backbone.
- Emulsifier molecules have both hydrophilic and hydrophobic parts.
- Emulsifiers are widely used in the food industry.

Proteins

In this section you have learned:

- Proteins are the major structural materials of animal tissue and are also involved in the maintenance and regulation of life processes.
- Proteins are condensation polymers made from amino acids.
- Amino acids contain an amino group ($-NH_2$) and a carboxyl group ($-COOH$).
- There are 20 different amino acids needed to make the proteins in our bodies.
- Some amino acids cannot be made in the body and must be obtained from dietary proteins and are referred to as essential amino acids.
- Given the structure of amino acids, show how they join to form part of a protein structure.
- The link joining amino acids is a peptide (amide) link.
- The long-chain molecules within proteins form spirals and sheets.
- The long-chain molecules are held together by intermolecular bonding.
- Proteins change shape (denature) when heated because the intermolecular bonds are broken.
- Most enzymes are proteins and act as biological catalysts.
- During digestion enzymes break proteins into amino acids.
- The breakdown of proteins during digestion is an example of hydrolysis.
- The structural formulae of amino acids obtained on hydrolysis of protein can be identified from the protein structure.

Oxidation of food

In this section you have learned:

- Aldehydes and ketones contain the carbonyl functional group.
- The carbonyl group has the structure

- In aldehydes the carbonyl functional group is on an end carbon.
- Many flavour molecules are aldehydes.
- In ketones the carbonyl functional group is joined to two other carbons.
- Given the systematic name for straight- and branched-chain aldehydes and ketones with up to eight carbons in the main chain, a structural formula can be drawn and molecular formula written.
- Given the structure for straight- and branched-chain aldehydes and ketones with up to eight carbons in the main chain, it can be systematically named.
- Aldehydes and ketones exhibit isomerism.
- The carbonyl functional group is polar and leads to permanent dipole–permanent dipole attractions between molecules.
- The boiling points of aldehydes and ketones are lower than those of equivalent alcohols which have hydrogen bonding.
- Low molecular mass aldehydes and ketones are water soluble due to hydrogen bonds forming between the carbonyl group and the water molecules.
- Low molecular mass aldehydes and ketones are very volatile.
- Aldehydes, but not ketones, can be oxidised to carboxylic acids.
- Oxidation can be identified by an increase in the oxygen to hydrogen ratio going from reactants to products.
- Carboxylic acids can be reduced to aldehydes, which can then be reduced to primary alcohols.
- Reduction can be identified by a decrease in the oxygen to hydrogen ratio going from reactants to products.
- Aldehydes and ketones can be distinguished using acidified potassium dichromate, Fehling's solution or Tollens' reagent.
- Primary alcohols can be oxidised to aldehydes then carboxylic acids.
- Secondary alcohols can be oxidised ketones.
- Hot copper(II) oxide or acidified dichromate(V) solution can be used to oxidise alcohols.
- Tertiary alcohols cannot be oxidised.
- Oxidation is the major cause of food spoilage.
- Oxygen can react with the fatty acids in fats and oils causing them to become rancid.
- Antioxidants are molecules which prevent other substances from oxidising.
- Antioxidants can be identified as the substance being oxidised in a redox equation.

Fragrances

In this section you have learned:

- Fragrances can be due to essential oils in plants.
- Essential oils are concentrated extracts of the volatile, non-water soluble aroma compounds obtained from plants.
- Essential oils are used in perfumes, cosmetic products, cleaning products and as flavourings in food.
- Most essential oils contain terpenes.
- Terpenes are unsaturated compounds based on isoprene units joined together.
- The systematic name for isoprene is 2-methylbuta-1,3-diene.
- Isoprene units, including the number of units, can be identified in a terpene.
- The term terpene is used to include compounds containing different functional groups.
- Oxidation of terpenes in plants is responsible for the aroma of many spices.

Skin care

In this section you have learned:

- UV light is high-energy radiation which can break bonds within molecules forming free radicals which cause skin damage, including accelerated ageing of the skin.
- Sun blocks can physically protect by reflecting UV radiation.
- Free radicals are single atoms or groups of atoms with unpaired electrons and are very reactive and can initiate chain reactions.
- The three stages of a free radical chain reaction are initiation, propagation and termination.
- Initiation, propagation and termination steps in a free radical chain reaction can be shown in an equation.
- Free radical scavengers react with free radicals preventing free radical chain reactions taking place.
- Free radical scavengers are also known as antioxidants.
- Antioxidants are added to cosmetic products to prevent free radical damage to skin tissue.
- Antioxidants are added to foods to prevent them from spoiling and improve shelf life.
- Free radical scavengers are added to plastics to slow down degradation by UV light and oxygen.

Getting the most from reactants 1

Maximising profit

When making new products, industrial chemists have to think about the cheapest and most efficient way of doing so in order to maximise profit.

Key considerations are:

- **Availability**, **sustainability** (long-term supply) and **cost** of **feedstocks** – the chemicals that have to be reacted or processed in some way in order to make a product.
- **Product yield** – the quantity of chemical produced by a particular chemical process.
- **Marketability of by-products** – often there are other products formed in addition to the intended product, which can be used elsewhere in the process or sold to other companies and used rather than being wasted.
- **Recycling** – if unreacted chemicals and solvents can be fed back into the reactor, this improves the efficiency and profitability of the process as well as reducing potential environmental pollutants being released.
- **Energy requirements** – the cost of energy sources such as gas and electricity are steadily increasing, so low-energy processes are more profitable, and ways of using energy released during chemical reactions need to be found.

Case study – Ammonia and urea production in New Zealand

Ammonia and urea production in New Zealand, highlighting some of the ways the process is made as efficient as possible.

Minimising health risks and the impact on the environment

Industrial chemists have to think about health and safety issues to protect workers, the public and the environment in general. In recent years the chemical industry has become more aware of **green chemistry** – the design of chemical products and processes that reduce or eliminate the use and production of hazardous substances.

The main principles of green chemistry are:

1. Waste prevention.

2. More energy-efficient processes with fewer steps and fewer by-products improve the atom economy (see page 75).

3. Use of fewer hazardous and toxic chemicals.

4. Safer processes and products.

5. Design products which can be degraded in the environment.

6. Use of more specific catalysts, such as enzymes which reduce energy requirements.

Many pharmaceutical companies use enzyme catalysts to help achieve green chemistry ideals:

Many conventional industrial processes were inefficient and paid little attention to environmental effects.

Green industrial processes both use and produce fewer toxic chemicals, and pay greater attention to the environment.

> ### TOP TIP
> Although it is important that industrial chemists make products as cheaply as possible, they have to ensure that health and safety and environmental issues are addressed.

Quick Test 25

1. An industrial chemical manufacturer wants to adapt one of its processes so it becomes more 'green'. Outline the areas which need to be examined to achieve this.

Getting the most from reactants 2

Measuring the efficiency of a reaction

Manufacturers aim to use chemical reactions and processes that make the most effective use of available resources, while generating the smallest possible amount of waste material. The efficiency of a process can be measured by calculating the **percentage yield** and **atom economy**.

> **TOP TIP**
>
> Atom economy is calculated in the planning stage, but yield can only be found experimentally.

Percentage yield

Yield is the final, usable product of a process. Percentage yield compares the expected product quantity with the actual amount produced. The expected or theoretical yield is calculated from the balanced equation. You can find out how to calculate the theoretical yield on page 79.

$$\text{Percentage yield} = \frac{\text{actual yield}}{\text{theoretical yield}} \times 100$$

Example

Aspirin is a well-known painkiller made from salicylic acid:

$$C_7H_6O_3 \ + \ C_4H_6O_3 \ \rightarrow \ C_9H_8O_4 \ + \ C_2H_4O_2$$
$$\text{salicylic acid} \qquad\qquad \text{aspirin}$$

The theoretical yield of aspirin when 100 g of salicylic acid is reacted is 130·4 g. The actual yield is 121·2 g. Calculate the percentage yield of aspirin.

Worked answer:

$$\text{Percentage yield} = \frac{\text{actual yield}}{\text{theoretical yield}} \times 100$$
$$= \frac{121\cdot2}{130\cdot4} \times 100$$
$$= 92\cdot9\%$$

This is a very high yield, so – using this as an indicator – the process could be considered to be efficient.

Atom economy

The atom economy compares the proportion of reactant atoms that end up in a useful product compared to the number that end up as waste. This is one of the key ideas in green chemistry. Atom economy can be calculated using the following equation:

$$\text{Atom economy (\%)} = \frac{\text{mass of desired product}}{\text{total mass of reactants}} \times 100$$

Example

Calculate the atom economy for the production of aspirin in the reaction:

$$C_7H_6O_3 \quad + \quad C_4H_6O_3 \quad \rightarrow \quad C_9H_8O_4 \quad + \quad C_2H_4O_2$$

salicylic acid   aspirin   ethanoic acid

Formula mass: 138   102   180   60

Worked answer:

$$\text{Atom economy (\%)} = \frac{\text{mass of desired product}}{\text{total mass of reactants}} \times 100$$

$$= \frac{180}{240} \times 100$$

$$= 75\%$$

Using atom economy as a measure of reaction efficiency, this reaction would be considered high. If the by-products of a reaction can be used, the atom economy is improved, and therefore the overall efficiency can be considered to be even higher.

In this reaction the other product is ethanoic acid, which is a useful product and therefore not wasted, so the reaction atom economy could be considered to be 100%.

TOP TIP

The relationships for calculating percentage yield and atom economy are given in the SQA data booklet.

TOP TIP

Both percentage yield and atom economy have to be considered when working out the efficiency of a chemical process. A reaction which has a high yield may have a poor atom economy if there are a number of by-products, so is not as efficient as it might at first seem.

Calculating the cost

If the cost of the feedstocks and the percentage yield for a reaction are known, then the cost of the reactants used in the reaction can be calculated.

Example

In the worked example on page 74, the percentage yield of aspirin from salicylic acid was calculated as 92·9%. If the average cost of salicylic acid is £4·90/kg, calculate the cost of the salicylic acid to produce 100 g of aspirin.

$$C_7H_6O_3 \quad + \quad C_4H_6O_3 \quad \rightarrow \quad C_9H_8O_4 \quad + \quad C_2H_4O_2$$

Formula mass: 138   102   180   60

Worked answer:

Step 1: Calculate the mass of salicylic acid needed to produce 1 g of aspirin if the reaction is 100% efficient.

	$C_7H_6O_3$	+	$C_4H_6O_3$	$\rightarrow$	$C_9H_8O_4$	+	$C_2H_4O_2$
Key relationship	1 mol			$\rightarrow$	1 mol		
Convert to gram formula mass (GFM)	138 g			$\rightarrow$	180 g		
So	$\dfrac{138}{180}$ g			$\rightarrow$	1 g		
So	$\left(\dfrac{138}{180}\right) \times 100$			$\rightarrow$	100 g		

So theoretically 76·7 g of salicylic acid produces 100 g of aspirin.

Step 2: Calculate the mass of reactant needed given the % yield of the reaction.

The percentage yield is 92·9 %, so the mass of salicylic acid needed to produce 100 g of aspirin is $\dfrac{100}{92·9} \times 76·7 = 82·6$ g.

Step 3: Calculate the actual cost of the reactant.

1000 g of salicylic acid costs £4·90, so 82·6 g costs $\dfrac{82·6}{1000} \times £4·90 = £0·40$.

TOP TIP

The mass of a mole of any substance, in grams (g), is equal to the gram formula mass (GFM) and can be calculated using relative atomic masses.

Why the yield is not 100%

There are several reasons:

1. The reaction may not go to completion: some of the reactants are not converted into products.
2. Side-reactions, that produce by-products, may occur.
3. Difficulty in purifying the product which can lead to loss of product.

Quick Test 26

1. Ammonia is made industrially by the Haber process: $N_2 + 3H_2 \rightleftharpoons 2NH_3$

   When 112 g of nitrogen is reacted with hydrogen, the theoretical yield of ammonia is 136 g. The actual yield is 40·8 g.

   (a) Calculate the percentage yield of ammonia.

   (b) What is the atom economy for the reaction?

   (c) Comment on the overall efficiency of the reaction.

2. Phenol (C_6H_5OH) is an important industrial chemical which can be made from benzene (C_6H_6) as follows:

$$C_6H_6 + H_2SO_4 + 2NaOH \rightarrow C_6H_5OH + Na_2SO_3 + 2H_2O$$

   78 g of benzene should theoretically produce 94 g of phenol. The actual yield is 75 g.

   (a) Calculate the percentage yield of phenol.

   (b) Calculate the atom economy for the production of phenol.

   (c) Comment on the overall efficiency of the reaction.

3. The percentage yield of iron produced from iron ore is 79%. If the average cost of iron ore (Fe_2O_3) is £83 per tonne, calculate the cost of the iron ore needed to produce each tonne of iron (to the nearest £). (1 tonne = 1000 kg.)

$$\text{Balanced equation: } Fe_2O_3 + 3CO \rightarrow 2Fe + 3CO_2$$

Getting the most from reactants 3

Mole ratios in a formula

One mole of any substance contains the same number of **atoms** or **molecules** in an element as there are **molecules** or **ionic units** in a compound.

For example, 1 mole of aluminium has the same number of atoms as there are molecules in 1 mole of chlorine and 1 mole of carbon dioxide, and ionic units in 1 mole of sodium chloride.

One mole of molecules contains more than 1 mole of atoms.

For example, 1 mole of carbon dioxide (CO_2) contains 3 moles of atoms – 1 mole of carbon atoms and 2 moles of oxygen atoms. So, 0·5 moles of carbon dioxide contains 0·5 moles of carbon atoms and 1 mole of oxygen atoms, i.e. 1·5 moles of atoms.

One mole of ionic units has more than 1 mole of ions.

For example, 1 mole of sodium chloride (NaCl) contains 1 mole of Na^+ ions and 1 mole of Cl^- ions, i.e. 2 moles of ions in total. So, 0·5 moles of sodium chloride contains 0·5 moles of Na^+ ions and 0·5 moles of Cl^- ions, i.e. 1 mole of ions in total.

This relationship can be used to calculate masses of substances present in everyday foodstuffs.

Example

The nutritional information label on a packet of 'cup-a-soup' stated that it contained 0·55 g of sodium. The sodium is in the form of sodium chloride (NaCl).

Calculate the mass of sodium chloride in the packet of soup.

Worked answer:

Step 1: Calculate the number of moles of sodium ions – this is also the number of moles of NaCl ionic units.

GFM of Na = 23 g.

Number of moles of Na = $\dfrac{mass}{GFM}$

$$= \frac{0.55}{23} = 0.024 \text{ mol}$$

The number of moles of NaCl is also 0·024.

GFM of NaCl = 23·0 + 35·5 = 58·5 g.

Nutrition information		
Made up as per instructions		
Typical values	Per 100ml (as consumed)	Per Sachet (as consumed)
Energy	173kJ	387kJ
	(41kcal)	(92kcal)
Protein	0·5g	1·2g
Carbohydrates	7·2g	16·1g
of which sugar	1·4g	3·1g
Fat	1·1g	2·4g
of which saturates	0·9g	1·9g
Fibre	0·2g	0·5g
Sodium	0·25g	0·55g
	(250mg)	(550mg)

The nutritional information label from a soup packet showing the amount of sodium present.

Step 2: Calculate the mass of NaCl from the number of moles.

Mass = moles × GFM

$$= 0.024 \times 58.5 = 1.40 \text{ g}$$

So, the mass of sodium chloride in the packet of soup is 1·40 g.

Calculating masses reacting and produced

Quantities reacting and being produced can be calculated from balanced equations. We can do this because 1 mole of any substance contains the same number of atoms or molecules in an element, and molecules or ionic units in a compound.

The numbers in front of a formula in an equation tell us the number of **moles** reacting and being produced. The number 1 is never written in front of a formula in an equation – the fact that a formula is written tells you there must be at least 1 mole present.

The values obtained from the balanced equation are the theoretical values. The actual values are obtained by experiment.

> **TOP TIP**
>
> The theoretical yield calculated from the balanced equation is used along with the actual yield to calculate the percentage yield (see page 74).

Example

Calculate the theoretical mass of silver produced when 3·2 g of zinc metal is reacted with excess silver(I) nitrate solution.

Worked answer:

	Zn	$+$	$2AgNO_3$	$\rightarrow$	$2Ag$	$+$	$Zn(NO_3)_2$
	1 mol		2 mol		2 mol		1 mol
Key relationship	**1 mol**			$\rightarrow$	**2 mol**		
Converting to GFM:	65·4 g			$\rightarrow$	215·8 g (2 × 107·9)		
So	1·0 g $\frac{65·4}{65·4}$			$\rightarrow$	3·3 g $\frac{215·8}{65·4}$		
So	3·2 g (1 × 3·2)			$\rightarrow$	7·82 g (3·3 × 3·2) = 10·56		

The mass of silver produced is 10·56 g.

> **TOP TIP**
>
> Actual mass of a desired product in a chemical reaction will be less than the theoretical values because: by-products could form, the reaction may not go to completion, and reactants may not be pure.

> **TOP TIP**
>
> If the answer was asked for in moles instead of grams, convert to moles using: moles $(n) = \frac{\text{mass (m)}}{\text{GFM}}$.
>
> This relationship can be found in the SQA data booklet.

Quick Test 27

1. The nutritional information label on a family bag of potato crisps stated that it contained 0·82 g of sodium. The sodium is in the form of sodium chloride (NaCl). Calculate the mass of sodium chloride in the bag of potato crisps.

2. Calculate the mass of copper produced when 1·7 g of copper(I) sulfide is roasted in the air.

$$Cu_2S(s) + O_2(g) \rightarrow 2Cu(s) + SO_2(g)$$

Getting the most from reactants 4

Calculating the number of moles of solution reacting and produced from a balanced equation

TOP TIP

The relationship between concentration (c), moles (n) and volume (V) is given in the SQA data booklet as $n = c \times V$.

Example

Calculate the number of **moles** of sodium hydroxide needed to completely neutralise 150 cm³ of 0·1 mol l⁻¹ sulfuric acid.

$$2NaOH + H_2SO_4 \rightarrow Na_2SO_4 + 2H_2O$$

Worked answer:

Work out the key mole relationship from the balanced equation.

$$2NaOH + H_2SO_4 \rightarrow Na_2SO_4 + 2H_2O$$

2 mol　　　**1 mol**

Key relationship

From the question, 150 cm³ of 0·1 mol l⁻¹ sulfuric acid reacts completely.

Calculate number of moles: $n = c \times V$

$$= 0·10 \times 0·15$$

$$= 0·015 \text{ mol}$$

The mole ratio shows that **twice** the number of moles of sodium hydroxide are needed to completely neutralise the sulfuric acid, i.e. **0·03** mol.

Calculating the concentration of a reactant from a balanced equation

Example

Calculate the concentration of a sodium hydroxide solution if 50 cm³ of the solution were needed to neutralise 150 cm³ of 0·1 mol l⁻¹ sulfuric acid.

Worked answer:

Step 1: Calculate the number of moles of sulfuric acid reacting, and so the number of moles of sodium hydroxide needed, as done in the example above: **0·03** mol.

Step 2: Calculate the concentration of the sodium hydroxide:

$$c = \frac{n}{V}$$

$$\text{So } c = \frac{0.03}{0.05} = \mathbf{0.6} \text{ mol } l^{-1}$$

TOP TIP

If you are asked to 'show your working clearly' you must do so or you will lose marks. It is also helpful for you to lay out your working in a logical way, setting out each step. This also helps you to avoid putting the wrong figures into your calculator.

Calculating the volume of solution needed for complete reaction from a balanced equation

Example

Calculate the **volume** of 0·1 mol l^{-1} sodium hydroxide solution needed to neutralise 150 cm³ of 0·1 mol l^{-1} sulfuric acid.

$$2NaOH + H_2SO_4 \rightarrow Na_2SO_4 + 2H_2O$$

Worked answer:

Step 1: Calculate the number of moles of sulfuric acid reacting, and so the number of moles of sodium hydroxide needed, as done in the example on page 80: **0·03** mol.

Step 2: Calculate the volume from the number of moles.

$$V = \frac{n}{c}$$

$$\text{So } V = \frac{0.03}{0.1} = \mathbf{0.30} \text{ l } (300 \text{ cm}^3)$$

Quick Test 28

1. Calculate the number of **moles** of sodium hydroxide solution needed to neutralise 20 cm³ of 0·1 mol l^{-1} sulfuric acid.

    $$2NaOH + H_2SO_4 \rightarrow Na_2SO_4 + 2H_2O$$

2. 17·8 cm³ of potassium hydroxide solution is required to completely neutralise 40 cm³ of 0·1 mol l^{-1} hydrochloric acid. Calculate the **concentration** of the potassium hydroxide solution.

    $$KOH + HCl \rightarrow KCl + H_2O$$

3. Calculate the **volume** of 0·25 mol l^{-1} lithium hydroxide needed to completely neutralise 25 cm³ of 0·1 mol l^{-1} sulfuric acid.

    $$2LiOH + H_2SO_4 \rightarrow Li_2SO_4 + 2H_2O$$

Getting the most from reactants 5

Reactants in excess

It is seldom the case that all of the reactants actually react to form products. One reactant is usually completely used up – this is the **limiting reactant**. Other reactants that are not completely used up are in **excess**. Calculations must be based on the quantity of the limiting reactant present.

Example

25 cm^3 of 0·2 mol l^{-1} potassium hydroxide solution is added to 15 cm^3 of 0·5 mol l^{-1} hydrochloric acid.

$$KOH + HCl \rightarrow KCl + H_2O$$

Show by calculation which reactant is in excess.

Worked answer:

Step 1: Work out the **key mole relationship** from the balanced equation.

$$KOH + HCl \rightarrow KCl + H_2O$$

Key relationship   **1 mol**   **1 mol**

Step 2: Calculate the **number of moles** of each reactant from the information in the question:

moles (n)   = concentration (c) × volume (V)

KOH: moles = 0·2 × 0·025

           = 0·0050 mol

HCl: moles = 0·5 × 0·015

           = 0·0075 mol

The potassium hydroxide and hydrochloric acid react in a 1:1 ratio, so the hydrochloric acid is in excess by 0·0025 mol (0·0075 – 0·0050) and the potassium hydroxide is the limiting reactant.

TOP TIP

The mole ratios from the balanced equation are key to calculating the number of moles of each chemical reacting.

TOP TIP

In industry, to ensure that a costly reactant is converted into product, an excess of the less expensive reactant(s) can be used.

Example

Hydrogen gas can be produced in the laboratory by reacting magnesium with hydrochloric acid. 1·6 g of magnesium was added to 250 cm³ of 0·5 mol l⁻¹ hydrochloric acid.

Calculate which reactant is in excess.

$$Mg + 2HCl \rightarrow MgCl_2 + H_2$$

Worked answer:

Step 1: Work out the **key mole relationship** from the balanced equation.

$$Mg + 2HCl \rightarrow MgCl_2 + H_2$$
$$1 \text{ mol} \quad 2 \text{ mol}$$

Step 2: Calculate the **number of moles** of each reactant from the information in the question.

Magnesium: moles (n) $= \dfrac{\text{mass (m)}}{\text{GFM}}$

$= \dfrac{1 \cdot 6}{24 \cdot 3}$

$= 0 \cdot 066$ mol

Acid: moles (n) $=$ concentration (c) × volume (V)

$= 0 \cdot 5 \times 0 \cdot 25$

$= 0 \cdot 125$ mol

> **TOP TIP**
>
> The volume of hydrogen gas produced can be calculated and this is covered in **Getting the most from reactants 7**.

Because the mole ratio of magnesium:acid is 1:2, the number of moles of acid needed to react with all of the magnesium would be 2 × 0·066 = 0·132 mol. There is only 0·125 mol of acid available, so the acid is the limiting reactant, and the magnesium is in excess by 0·0035 mol (0·0660 − 0·0625).

Quick Test 29

1.　1·1 g of calcium carbonate is added to 100 cm³ of 0·25 mol l⁻¹ hydrochloric acid.

$$CaCO_3 + 2HCl \rightarrow CaCl_2 + H_2O + CO_2$$

　(a) Calculate which reactant is in excess, and by how much.

　(b) Calculate the mass of calcium chloride produced.

2.　5·9 g of copper metal is added to 250 cm³ of 0·5 mol l⁻¹ silver(I) nitrate solution.

$$Cu + 2AgNO_3 \rightarrow Cu(NO_3)_2 + 2Ag$$

　(a) Calculate which reactant is in excess, and by how much.

　(b) Calculate the mass of silver produced.

Getting the most from reactants 6

TOP TIP

For gases, **1 mol = molar volume**. The unit for molar volume is **litres mol⁻¹ (l mol⁻¹)**.

Molar volume

Molar volume (V_m) is the volume occupied by one mole of a gas when measured at a given temperature and pressure. This means that the molar volume changes depending on the temperature and pressure at which it is measured. The molar volume for **any** gas is the same so long as it is measured at the same temperature and pressure. Measured at standard temperature and pressure (s.t.p. = 0°C and 1 atmosphere pressure) molar volume is 22·4 l mol⁻¹. Measured at room temperature and pressure (20°C and 1 atmosphere pressure) molar volume is approximately 24·0 l mol⁻¹.

Calculating volumes of gas

If the molar volume is known then the volume occupied by a quantity of gas can be calculated.

Example

Calculate the volume occupied by 0·3 mol of methane at room temperature and pressure.

$$V_m = 24 \cdot 0 \text{ l mol}^{-1}$$

Worked answer:

$$1 \text{ mol} = 24 \cdot 0 \text{ l mol}^{-1}$$

$$\text{So} \quad 0 \cdot 3 \text{ mol} = 0 \cdot 3 \times 24 \cdot 0 = 7 \cdot 2 \text{ l}$$

Example

Calculate the volume occupied by 2·3 g of carbon dioxide.

$$V_m = 23 \cdot 8 \text{ l mol}^{-1}$$

Worked answer:

Step 1: Convert mass to moles.

$$\text{Moles} = \frac{\text{mass}}{\text{GFM}}$$

$$= 2 \cdot 3 / 44 \cdot 0$$

$$= 0 \cdot 052 \text{ mol}$$

Step 2: Convert moles to volume.

$$1 \text{ mol} = 23 \cdot 8 \text{ l mol}^{-1}$$

$$\text{So } 0 \cdot 052 \text{ mol} = 0 \cdot 052 \times 23 \cdot 8 = 1 \cdot 24 \text{ l}$$

TOP TIP

Converting mass to volume and volume to mass can be done by converting first to moles. Gram formula mass (GFM) ↔ 1 mole ↔ molar volume (V_m).

Example

Calculate the mass of 6·3 l of hydrogen.

$$V_m = 23\cdot9 \text{ l mol}^{-1}$$

Worked answer:

Step 1: Calculate the **moles** of hydrogen.

23·9 l is the volume occupied by 1 mol of H_2

6·3 l will be the volume occupied by $\dfrac{6\cdot3 \times 1}{23\cdot9} = 0\cdot264$ mol

Step 2: Calculate the mass from the number of moles.

$$1 \text{ mol} = 2 \text{ g}$$

$$\text{So } 0\cdot264 \text{ mol} = 2 \times 0\cdot264 = 0\cdot528 \text{ g}$$

Quick Test 30

1. In each part of the question take the molar volume to be 23·7 l mol^{-1}.
    (a) Calculate the volume occupied by 0·15 mol of helium gas.
    (b) Calculate the volume occupied by 0·32 g of helium.
    (c) A weather balloon was filled with 58·4 l of helium gas. Calculate the mass of the helium in the balloon.

Getting the most from reactants 7

Volumes reacting and being produced

Volumes of gas reacting and being produced can be calculated if the mole ratios of reactants and products from the balanced equation are known.

Example

Calculate the volume of carbon dioxide gas produced when 250 cm³ of propane (C_3H_8) burns in excess oxygen.

$$C_3H_8(g) + 5O_2(g) \rightarrow 3CO_2(g) + 4H_2O(\ell)$$

Worked answer:

Step 1: Work out the **key mole relationship** from the balanced equation.

$$C_3H_8(g) + 5O_2(g) \rightarrow 3CO_2(g) + 4H_2O(\ell)$$

Key relationship   1 mol   3 mol

Step 2: Use the relationship 1 mol = V_m. This means that if one gas volume is known, and the mole ratio is known, then the other gas volumes can be calculated by proportion.

$$C_3H_8(g) + 5O_2(g) \rightarrow 3CO_2(g) + 4H_2O(\ell)$$

              1 mol   3 mol

(vol is the volume of   1 vol   3 vol
gas given in the question)

       250 cm³ $\rightarrow$ 750 cm³

So 250 cm³ of methane produces 750 cm³ of carbon dioxide.

The question states that there is excess oxygen available, which means there is more than enough available to react with all of the propane. The exact volume of oxygen can be worked out from the mole ratio in the balanced equation – in this case 1:5, so the volume of oxygen used up is 1250 cm³.

Volumes of gas produced in reactions

When solids and solutions are involved in a reaction, it is possible to calculate the gas volumes produced.

You need to know the mole ratios from the balanced equation, and then calculate the number of moles actually being produced, lastly converting to volume.

Example

Calculate the volume of hydrogen gas produced when 0·75 g of magnesium reacts completely with excess hydrochloric acid. Take molar volume (V_m) to be 23·9 l mol^{-1}.

$$Mg + 2HCl \rightarrow MgCl_2 + H_2$$

Worked answer:

Step 1: Work out the key mole relationship from the balanced equation.

$$Mg + 2HCl \rightarrow MgCl_2 + H_2$$

1 mol	$\rightarrow$	1 mol
1 mol	$\rightarrow$	V_m (23·9 l mol^{-1})

Step 2: Calculate the moles of magnesium reacting.

$$Moles\ (n) = \frac{mass\ (m)}{GFM}$$
$$= \frac{0·75}{24·3}$$
$$= 0·031\ mol$$

Step 3: Calculate the volume of gas produced from the mole:V_m ratio in step 2.

$$1\ mol \rightarrow V_m\ (23·9\ l\ mol^{-1})$$
$$So\ 0·031\ mol \rightarrow 0·031 \times 23·9 = \mathbf{0·74\ l}$$

Quick Test 31

1. Butane gas (C_4H_{10}) is used as a portable fuel. It burns to produce carbon dioxide and water.

    $$C_4H_{10}(g) + \frac{13}{2}O_2(g) \rightarrow 4CO_2(g) + 5H_2O(\ell)$$

    (a) Calculate the volume of carbon dioxide produced when 125 cm^3 of butane is burned in excess oxygen.

    (b) Calculate the volume of oxygen which would be left if 1 l of oxygen was mixed with 100 cm^3 of butane and the mixture ignited.

2. Look at the example on page 83 in **Getting the most from reactants 5**. Calculate the volume of hydrogen gas produced when all of the acid reacts. (Take molar volume to be 23·9 l mol^{-1}.)

Controlling the rate of reaction 1

The importance of the rate of reaction

Generally speaking, industrial chemists want to speed up chemical reactions. They need to know how fast they can make a reaction go – typically, the faster the better. A reaction which is too slow is unlikely to be a commercial success. However, if the rate of reaction is too rapid there is the risk of explosion.

The rates of chemical reactions are affected by:

- the concentration of dissolved reactants and the pressure in gas reactions
- the size of solid reactant particles
- the collision geometry – the angle at which reactants collide.

The effect of each of these factors can be explained by collision theory.

Collision theory

Simple **collision theory** states that for reactants to form products, they must first come in contact with each other (collide).

The reaction of marble chips (calcium carbonate) with hydrochloric acid can be used to illustrate some of the effects:

calcium carbonate + hydrochloric acid → calcium chloride + water + carbon dioxide

$$CaCO_3(s) \quad + \quad 2HCl(aq) \quad \rightarrow \quad CaCl_2(aq) \quad + H_2O(\ell) + \quad CO_2(g)$$

TOP TIP

The more collisions that take place between reactant particles, the greater the chance of products being formed.

Concentration: the higher the concentration of the acid, the faster the reaction. The more particles there are, the more collisions there will be, and the greater the chance of reaction and products being formed. So, the higher the concentration, the more collisions and the faster the reaction.

Increasing the **pressure** in some reactions involving gases has a similar effect to increasing the concentration of the reactants. The gas molecules are compressed into a smaller space as the pressure is increased, so there is a greater chance of them colliding and going on to form products.

low concentration:
few particles in a given volume

high concentration:
many particles in the same volume

Particle size: the smaller the particle size, the faster the reaction. When equal masses of small lumps and large lumps are reacted with the same concentration of acid, the small lumps react more quickly.

 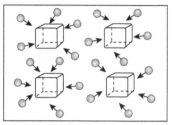

A large lump of solid has quite a small surface area. The reaction can only happen at the outside surface.

Smaller lumps of solid have a larger surface area at which the reaction can happen. The reaction rate is much faster.

Collision geometry

Not all collisions between reactants lead to products. One reason for this is the angle at which the molecules collide – the **collision geometry**. If two diatomic molecules collide end-on, this would not be the best alignment to form molecules of product. A better collision geometry would be if the molecules collided side-on or even end-to-side.

(a)

reactant molecules approach each other

ineffective collision – no reaction

reactants separate – no product

(b)

reactant molecules approach each other

effective collision – molecules have correct geometry

product molecules formed

Quick Test 32

1. Explain clearly the following observations:

    (a) increasing the concentration of nitric acid increases the speed at which it reacts with zinc metal;

    (b) powdered zinc reacts faster than lumps of zinc with nitric acid.

2. With the aid of diagrams, explain how collision geometry can affect the rate of a chemical reaction.

Controlling the rate of reaction 2

Temperature and activation energy

For many reactions, the higher the temperature, the faster the rate of reaction.

Acid warmed to 30°C will react much faster with marble chips than would acid at room temperature (approximately 20°C). Temperature is a measure of the average kinetic energy of the reactants. As the temperature increases, the kinetic energy of the reactants increases, i.e. they move faster. This results in more collisions taking place at a greater speed, so the chance of reactants forming products increases, and therefore the rate of reaction increases. However, a small rise in temperature (10°C) almost doubles the rate at which the acid reacts with the marble chips. This remarkable increase cannot be explained by an increase in the number of collisions, which is already high. The answer is that not only do collisions have to occur, but they have to have a minimum amount of kinetic energy, known as the **activation energy (E_a)**. This is the minimum energy required to overcome the repulsion of the outer electrons.

The need for activation energy explains why the rate of some reactions is very slow unless energy is supplied:

- When natural gas in the laboratory mixes with the air, there is no visible sign that a reaction is occurring, although many collisions are taking place. This is because so few molecules have the energy of activation. Sparking the gas/air mixture or holding a flame near it supplies the activation energy, so many more molecules can react. The activation energy for this reaction is high.

Energy distribution diagrams

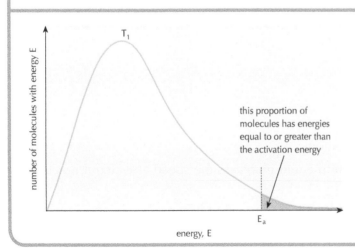

number of molecules with energy E

this proportion of molecules has energies equal to or greater than the activation energy

T_1

E_a

energy, E

Temperature can be considered to be a measure of the average kinetic energy of the particles in a substance. At a given temperature some particles will have high kinetic energy, and others low kinetic energy. Most particles will have kinetic energy somewhere in between. This can be displayed in an **energy distribution diagram**, as is shown opposite.

The total area under the graph shows the energy distribution of all the reactants at temperature T_1. Only a relatively small number of reactant particles have energy greater than the activation energy, E_a. This is shown as the shaded area under the graph.

If the temperature is increased, although there are the same number of particles, their energy distribution is different. More particles have higher kinetic energy. This is shown in the graph below, where the energy distribution at T_2 (higher than T_1) is superimposed on the diagram for temperature T_1.

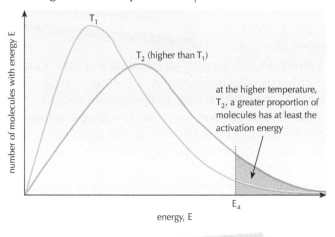

Notice that the shape of the graph at T_2 is distorted slightly to the right, to reflect that more particles have higher energy. The height of the graph is also lower than the graph at T_1. The shaded area under the graph shows that there are more than twice as many reactant particles with energy greater than E_a, so more than twice as many particles now have enough energy to react when they collide. This means that for a relatively small increase in temperature, there is a big increase in the rate of the reaction.

TOP TIP

A relatively small increase in temperature has a big effect on the rate of a reaction, because many more reacting molecules have energy equal to or greater than E_a.

Quick Test 33

1. In terms of activation energy, explain fully the reasoning behind advising people not to switch on lights or other electrical devices if they detect a gas leak.

2. The energy distribution diagram is for a reaction carried out at 40°C.

   (a) Add a line to the graph to show the energy distribution of the reactants if the reaction were carried out at 30°C.

   (b) Explain what the shaded area under the graph represents.

3. A student wrongly stated, 'The rate of a reaction increases when the temperature increases, because the activation energy increases, which increases the number of collisions.' Give the correct explanation.

Controlling the rate of reaction 3

Relative rate

The relationship between concentration and rate can be studied in more detail by carrying out a 'clock reaction'. This is where the effect of changing the concentration of one of the reactants in a reaction can be measured by timing how long it takes for a reaction to reach a certain point – usually indicated by a colour change. Because the concentration of only one reactant is being changed, the time it takes to reach the same point in the reaction must be due to the one reactant. The longer it takes to reach the same point in the reaction, the slower the rate. The rate of the reaction is inversely proportional to time (t), so can be taken as the reciprocal of time, i.e. 1/t, and is known as the relative rate (R).

A closer look at the effect of concentration on rate

A suitable clock reaction is hydrogen peroxide (H_2O_2) reacting with potassium iodide (KI) to form iodine (I_2).

$$H_2O_2(aq) + 2H^+(aq) + 2I^-(aq) \rightarrow 2H_2O(\ell) + I_2(aq)$$

The course of this reaction can be followed by carrying it out in the presence of small quantities of starch and thiosulfate ($S_2O_3^{2-}$) solutions. As the iodine molecules are produced, they immediately react with the thiosulfate ions and are converted back to colourless iodide ions:

$$I_2(aq) + 2S_2O_3^{2-}(aq) \rightarrow 2I^-(aq) + S_4O_6^{2-}(aq)$$

Once the thiosulfate ions have been used up, a blue/black colour suddenly appears, because the iodine molecules now have the opportunity to react with the starch. The time taken for the colour to first appear is noted.

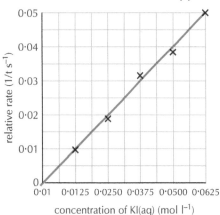

The graph is a straight line showing that rate is directly proportional to concentration, that is, if the concentration doubles, the rate doubles. This is the case for many chemical reactions.

A closer look at the effect of temperature on rate

The relationship between temperature and rate can be studied in more detail by studying the clock reaction between oxalic acid and acidified potassium permanganate:

$$5(COOH)_2(aq) + 6H^+(aq) + 2MnO_4^-(aq) \rightarrow 2Mn^{2+}(aq) + 10CO_2(g) + 8H_2O(\ell)$$

purple   colourless

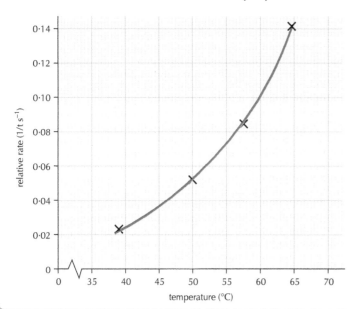

A series of experiments are carried out, in which only the temperature of the reaction mixtures is changed.

The graph, obtained from the results of such an experiment, shows that the rate is not directly proportional to temperature. A small rise in temperature results in a relatively large increase in rate. This supports the idea of activation energy.

Quick Test 34

1. (a) The reaction between hydrogen peroxide and potassium iodide was carried out using 0·190 mol l⁻¹ iodide solution. A sharp colour change was noted after 67 s.

    Calculate the relative rate of the reaction.

    (b) (i) From the graph of relative rate vs concentration, predict the relative rate when the concentration of the potassium iodide solution used is 0·125 mol l⁻¹.

    (ii) Justify your answer.

2. Look at the graph of relative rate against concentration.

    Calculate how long it would take before a colour change to blue/black would be seen if the concentration of the iodide solution was 0·0318 mol l⁻¹.

3. The reaction between oxalic acid and acidified permanganate solution was carried out at 25°C. The purple colour of the permanganate ion disappeared after 102 s.

    Calculate the relative rate of the reaction.

Controlling the rate of reaction 4

Interpreting rate graphs

The course of a reaction can be followed by measuring the volume of gas given off over time, and drawing a graph of volume of gas against time.

Experiment 1

A suitable experiment would be to observe the reaction of 40 cm³ of 0·2 mol l⁻¹ hydrochloric acid with excess magnesium ribbon at room temperature (20°C):

magnesium + hydrochloric acid → magnesium chloride + hydrogen

$$Mg(s) + 2HCl(aq) \rightarrow MgCl_2(aq) + H_2(g)$$

Interpreting the shape of the graph

At 1: The steepest part of the graph – the rate is at its highest. The maximum number of reactant particles are present, and the number of effective collisions per second is at its highest.

At 2: The graph is not so steep – the rate of reaction is slowing. Some of the reacting particles have been used up so the number of effective collisions per second is less.

At 3: The graph is horizontal – the reaction has stopped. The acid has been completely used up.

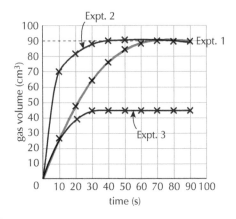

The graphs opposite are for the same reaction, but with some of the variables changed (quantities of reactant, particle size and temperature.) Expt. 1 (red line) are the original results.

TOP TIP

The slope of a graph indicates how fast the rate of reaction is. The steeper the slope, the faster the reaction.

Experiment 2

The reaction of 40 cm³ of 0·2 mol l⁻¹ hydrochloric acid with excess magnesium ribbon, but at a higher temperature than used in Experiment 1.

Interpreting the graph for Experiment 2

The graph is steeper than Experiment 1 initially, indicating that the reaction is faster. This is because the reaction is taking place at a higher temperature. More particles have energy greater than the activation energy. All the other variables are as in Experiment 1. The final volume of gas produced is the same as in Experiment 1, although it is produced faster in Experiment 2, because the mass of magnesium ribbon and the number of moles of acid reacting is the same.

Experiment 3

The reaction of 20 cm³ of 0·2 mol l⁻¹ hydrochloric acid with excess magnesium ribbon, at the same temperature used in Experiment 1.

Interpreting the graph for Experiment 3

The graph has the same slope as Experiment 1 initially, indicating that the rate of reaction is the same. This is because the concentration of the hydrochloric acid, the temperature, and the amount of magnesium ribbon are the same in both experiments. The final volume of gas obtained is half of that in Experiment 1 because the number of moles of acid reacting is half that of the original.

Quick Test 35

1. Experiment 1 was repeated using excess magnesium powder.

    (a) Sketch the graph for Experiment 1, and add a line to the graph for the experiment carried out with powdered magnesium.

    (b) Explain the shape of the graph you have drawn.

Controlling the rate of reaction 5

Reaction pathways

When chemical reactions occur, they are often accompanied by a significant change in energy. This is known as the **enthalpy change** and is given the symbol **ΔH**. ΔH is measured in **kJ** or **kJ mol^{-1}** when one mole of substance is reacted or produced.

When energy is released into the surrounding area (most commonly in the form of heat) the reaction is said to be **exothermic** and the value is given a negative sign. The energy released when new products are formed in an exothermic reaction must have come from the reactants, which have potential energy (PE). Some of this potential energy is released as heat during the reaction. Combustion and neutralisation are exothermic reactions, and so have negative ΔH values.

When energy is taken in from the surrounding area, the reaction is said to be **endothermic** and the value is given a positive sign.

Enthalpy changes can be shown in potential energy diagrams – the activation energy (E$_a$) is also shown in the diagrams.

If potential energy values are added to the diagrams, the enthalpy change (ΔH) for a reaction can be calculated by subtracting the enthalpy of the products from the enthalpy of the reactants:

$$\Delta H = H_{(products)} - H_{(reactants)}$$

The activation energy can be calculated by subtracting the enthalpy of the reactants from the energy maximum in the graph.

TOP TIP

In exothermic reactions, the PE of the products is less than the PE of the reactants. The 'missing' PE is given out as heat into the surrounding area. In endothermic reactions the PE of the products is greater than the PE of the reactants. The 'extra' PE is taken in from the surrounding area.

TOP TIP

Exothermic reactions always have a negative sign in front of the ΔH value to indicate the reaction is exothermic. Endothermic reactions should have a positive sign in front of the ΔH value – it is often missed out though.

Example

Calculate (i) the enthalpy change, and (ii) the activation energy from the potential energy diagram shown.

Worked answer:

(i) $\Delta H = H_{(products)} - H_{(reactants)}$

$= 100 - 300$

$\Delta H = -200$ kJ

(ii) $E_a = 450 - 300$

$E_a = 150$ kJ

The potential energy diagrams show the activation energy as an energy barrier, which the reactants have to overcome in order to form products. Reactant molecules with energy equal to or greater than the activation energy can go on to form products. Reactant molecules with energy lower than the activation energy will not go on to form products.

The lower the activation energy, the faster the rate of reaction.

The higher the activation energy, the slower the rate of reaction.

This explains why although petrol is very flammable, you can safely fill up a car's tank at the pump, because the activation energy needed for the combustion of petrol is high. It also explains why there are 'No Smoking' signs on display at petrol stations. A flame near petrol would supply the activation energy needed for combustion to occur.

Quick Test 36

1. (a) Calculate (i) the enthalpy change, and
        (ii) the activation energy from the potential energy diagram shown.

    (b) (i) Is the reaction exothermic or endothermic?

        (ii) Justify your answer.

2. Reactions (a) and (b) are associated with iron production:

    (a) $C(s) + O_2(g) \rightarrow CO_2(g)$ $\Delta H = -394$ kJ mol^{-1}

    (b) $C(s) + CO_2(g) \rightarrow 2CO(g)$ $\Delta H = +173$ kJ mol^{-1}

    (i) Sketch potential energy diagrams for both reactions (they do not have to be drawn to scale).

    (ii) Indicate the ΔH and E_a on each diagram.

    (iii) For each reaction, state whether it is exothermic or endothermic. Justify your choices.

Controlling the rate of reaction 6

The activated complex

As a reaction progresses there is a stage reached where an intermediate product is formed known as the **activated complex**. The top of the potential energy barrier represents the point at which the activated complex has formed.

The activation energy can be defined as the minimum energy needed by colliding particles to form the activated complex. Activated complexes are very unstable, and only exist for a short time. Not all activated complexes lose energy by going on to form products. They can break down to reform reactants. This is indicated by the arrows in the potential energy diagram.

The structure of many activated complexes is not known. When two diatomic molecules react, a 'square' activated complex can form – the dotted lines indicate bonds breaking and bonds forming.

Catalysts and activation energy

A catalyst is a substance which increases the rate of a particular reaction, without being used up in the reaction.

Catalysts are essential in many important industrial processes, some of which were covered in the National 5 course – these are summarised in the table below:

Process	Catalyst	Reaction
Haber – making ammonia	iron	$N_2 + 3H_2 \rightarrow 2NH_3$
Ostwald – making nitric acid	platinum	$4NH_3 + 5O_2 \rightarrow 4NO + 6H_2O$
Hydrogenation – making margarine	nickel	Unsaturated oils + $H_2 \rightarrow$ saturated fats

The catalyst acts as a site for the reaction to take place. If no catalyst were used, the reaction would take place via a different route and at a different rate. The steps in a catalyst-assisted pathway each have lower activation energy than the route without the catalyst, so more molecules have enough energy to react. This is shown in the potential energy diagram on page 99.

Potential energy diagram comparing the E_a of a catalysed reaction with the uncatalysed reaction

The catalysts in the table on page 98 work because the reactant molecules attach themselves temporarily to the surface of the catalyst.

Whenever a catalyst is used, its surface area is made as big as possible to provide a large area for collisions between the catalyst and reactant molecules. The catalyst is often referred to as 'finely divided'.

Quick Test 37

1. (a) An activated complex is formed during many reactions. Explain what is meant by 'activated complex'.

   (b) Two covalently bonded molecules, A-A and B-B, react to form a product, A-B.

   $$A_2 + B_2 \rightarrow 2AB$$

   Sketch the shape of a possible activated complex.

2. Catalytic converters in car exhaust systems use platinum to remove harmful gases.

   (a) Name the process which takes place at the surface of the catalyst.

   (b) Describe the process which takes place at the surface of the catalyst.

   (c) Explain why more molecules are able to react when a catalyst is used in a chemical reaction.

Chemical energy 1

Controlling the amount of heat

For industrial processes, chemists have to be able to calculate the amount of heat given out or taken in. Endothermic reactions require heat to be supplied and this is likely to push costs up. If a reaction is exothermic, the heat will have to be removed to prevent the temperature getting too high and causing thermal runaway.

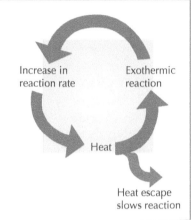

Increase in reaction rate

Exothermic reaction

Heat

Heat escape slows reaction

Thermal runaway refers to a situation where an increase in temperature changes the conditions in a way that causes a further increase in temperature. This causes the reaction to go out of control, and can often result in an explosion.

Most industrial reactions are exothermic, and nearly every large-scale chemical process has at least one step with the potential for thermal runaway, if the conditions are right. This means they must have a way of allowing heat to escape.

TOP TIP

Stored chemical energy is known as enthalpy. Remind yourself about enthalpy changes by looking at **Controlling the rate of reaction 5: Reaction pathways**.

Measuring enthalpy of combustion by experiment

At National 5, you learned how to calculate the quantity of heat energy released when a substance burns completely in oxygen. This is important when working out, for example, how effective a fuel a certain substance might be. To make a fair comparison, the enthalpy change when burning the same quantity of fuel should be compared. Enthalpy changes given in data books are for **one mole** of a substance burning completely at standard temperature (25°C) and pressure (1 atmosphere), all substances being in their standard states; this is known as the **standard enthalpy of combustion** (ΔH_c).

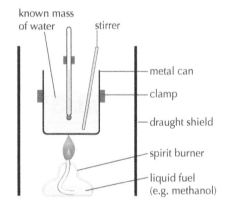

known mass of water

stirrer

metal can

clamp

draught shield

spirit burner

liquid fuel (e.g. methanol)

The diagram shows the arrangement which can be used to work out the enthalpy of combustion of methanol.

From the experimental results, the amount of energy transferred to the water (E_h) can be calculated by entering the values into a simple equation which connects them:

$$E_h = c \times m \times \Delta T$$

The change in temperature (ΔT) can be worked out by subtracting the final temperature from the initial temperature.

The mass of water (**m**), in kg, is known (1 cm³ = 1 g).

The energy needed to raise the temperature of 1 kg (1 litre) of water by 1°C [the specific heat capacity of water, (**c**)] is 4·18 kJ kg⁻¹ °C⁻¹. The value of c can be found in the SQA data booklet.

The mass of methanol burned is calculated by weighing the burner before and after the experiment.

The enthalpy of combustion can be calculated from the quantity of heat transferred to the water as shown in the example.

Example

0·68 g of methanol raises the temperature of 100 g of water in the metal can by 22·4°C. Calculate the enthalpy of combustion (ΔH_c) of methanol.

Worked answer:

Step 1: Work out the heat energy transferred to the water (E_h):

$$E_h = c \times m \times \Delta T$$
$$= 4\cdot18 \times 0\cdot1 \times 22\cdot4$$
$$E_h = 9\cdot36 \text{ kJ}$$

Step 2: Calculate the amount of fuel used, in moles $\left(n = \dfrac{m}{GFM}\right)$:
GFM of methanol (CH_3OH) = 32·0 g.

$$n = \frac{m}{GFM} = \frac{0\cdot68}{32\cdot0} = 0\cdot021 \text{ mol}$$

Step 3: Work out the energy transferred to the water when 1 mole of methanol burns, i.e. the enthalpy of combustion:

0·021 moles of methanol releases 9·36 kJ

So 1 mole of methanol releases $\dfrac{9\cdot36}{0\cdot021} = 445\cdot7$ kJ mol⁻¹.

So the enthalpy of combustion of methanol = –445·7 kJ mol⁻¹.

TOP TIP

The relationship $E_h = c \times m \times \Delta T$ is in the SQA data booklet, so you don't have to memorise it. The relationship can be rearranged so that c, m or ΔT can be calculated.

The standard enthalpy of combustion of methanol from the SQA data booklet is –726 kJ mol⁻¹. The experimental value for methanol is a fair bit lower than the standard value. This is because the experimental value is not obtained under standard conditions, and there are considerable heat losses to the surrounding area from the flame and the metal can. Therefore, not all the heat from the flame and the metal can reach the water.

TOP TIP

There is a – sign before the numerical value because the reaction is exothermic. The units are kJ mol⁻¹ because enthalpy of combustion is the energy released when 1 mole of methanol is burned.

Quick Test 38

1. (a) 0·38 g of propan-1-ol (C_3H_7OH) raises the temperature of 100 g of water in a metal can by 25·4°C. Calculate the enthalpy of combustion of propan-1-ol.

    (b) Suggest why the experimental results are less than the data booklet values.

2. 0·39 g of ethanol was burned and the heat produced used to heat 100 g of water. 8·33 kJ of energy was produced. Calculate the rise in temperature of the water, assuming all of the energy was transferred to the water.

Chemical energy 2

Heat energy released during neutralisation

An experiment can be carried out to collect data to calculate the quantity of heat energy released when an acid neutralises an alkali.

An example is the neutralisation reaction between hydrochloric acid and potassium hydroxide, which is an exothermic reaction:

hydrochloric acid + potassium hydroxide $\rightarrow$ water + potassium chloride

$HCl(aq)$ + $KOH(aq)$ $\rightarrow$ $H_2O(\ell)$ + $KCl(aq)$

The quantity of heat energy released can be determined in the laboratory using the simple calorimeter shown in the diagram opposite.

The experiment is carried out as follows:

thermometer reading to 0·1 °C

expanded polystyrene cup with lid

Step 1: Measure out separately known volumes of acid and alkali, measuring the temperature of each.

Step 2: Mix the acid with the alkali in a polystyrene cup, stir the mixture, and record the highest temperature reached.

Step 3: Calculate the change in temperature (ΔT) by subtracting the average temperature of the acid and alkali from the highest temperature recorded.

The quantity of heat energy released can be calculated using $E_h = c \times m \times \Delta T$. In this experiment the mass (m) is the combined volume of acid and alkali. Even though it is not pure water absorbing the heat produced, the specific heat capacity of water (c) is still used, i.e. 4·18 kJ kg⁻¹ °C⁻¹

The enthalpy change when one mole of water is formed can be calculated from the quantity of heat released during the experiment. This is shown in the example.

TOP TIP

When calculating the enthalpy change for any reaction, it is usually worked out for 1 mole of reactant or product.

Example

A group of students mixed 50 cm³ of 1·0 mol l⁻¹ hydrochloric acid with 50 cm³ of 1·0 mol l⁻¹ potassium hydroxide. The temperature rise was 6·3°C. Calculate: (a) the quantity of heat energy released and (b) enthalpy change when 1 mole of water is produced.

Worked answer:

(a) Work out the energy transferred to the water (E_h):
(m = 50 + 50 = 100 cm³ = 100 g = 0·1 kg)

$$E_h = c \times m \times \Delta T$$
$$= 4·18 \times 0·1 \times 6·3$$
$$E_h = 2·63 \text{ kJ}$$

(b) **Step 1:** Calculate the number of moles of acid (or alkali) used:

$$\text{Moles (n) = concentration (c) × volume (V)}$$
$$= 1·0 \times 0·05$$
$$= 0·05 \text{ mol}$$

We know that the reaction taking place is:

$$H^+ (aq) \ + \ OH^- (aq) \ \rightarrow \ H_2O(\ell)$$

From the balanced equation:

	1 mol	1 mol →	1 mol
So	0·05 mol	0·05 mol	0·05 mol
So	0·05 mol of water is formed.		

Step 2: Work out the energy transferred when 1 mole of water is formed:

When 0·05 moles of water is formed, the energy released is 2·63 kJ

So, when 1 mole of water is formed, the enthalpy change is
$$\frac{2·63}{0·05} = -52·7 \text{ kJ mol}^{-1}.$$

> ### TOP TIP
> The actual value for the enthalpy change when 1 mole of water is formed in a neutralisation reaction is −57·2 kJ mol⁻¹. The difference in values is mainly due to heat loss to the surroundings during the laboratory experiment. The value is the same for any acid and alkali reacting because the same reaction is happening each time, i.e. water is produced.

Quick Test 39

1. A group of students mixed 25 cm³ of 1·0 mol l⁻¹ hydrochloric acid with 25 cm³ of 1·0 mol l⁻¹ sodium hydroxide. The temperature rise was 6·4°C.

$$HCl(aq) + NaOH(aq) \rightarrow H_2O(\ell) + NaCl(aq)$$

Calculate the enthalpy change when 1 mole of water is produced.

2. Explain why the enthalpy change when 1 mol of water is formed in a neutralisation reaction is the same, no matter which acid or alkali is used.

Chemical energy 3

Energy cycles and Hess's law

Some enthalpies of reaction can be measured experimentally. However, many cannot, so an indirect approach using energy cycles is used.

Using energy cycles to work out an enthalpy of reaction relies on **Hess's law**, which states that the enthalpy change for a chemical reaction is independent of the route taken from reactants to products, so long as the starting and finishing conditions are the same for each route. This is shown in an energy cycle in the diagram opposite:

The overall enthalpy change for route 2 must be the same as for route 1:

$$\Delta H_1 = \Delta H_2 + \Delta H_3 + \Delta H_4$$

We can use this idea to work out the enthalpy of formation of methane:

$$C(s) + 2H_2(g) \rightarrow CH_4(g) \ \Delta H_f \ \text{(target equation)}$$

Methane cannot be made directly from its elements, carbon and hydrogen, but Hess's law can be used to calculate the enthalpy of formation by an indirect route. We can devise an energy cycle using enthalpies of combustion of carbon, hydrogen and methane to calculate the enthalpy of formation.

The equations for the combustion of carbon, hydrogen and methane are shown below (the enthalpies of combustion are from the SQA data booklet):

$$C(s) + O_2(g) \rightarrow CO_2(g) \qquad \Delta H_1 = -394 \ kJ \ mol^{-1}$$

$$H_2(g) + \tfrac{1}{2}O_2(g) \rightarrow H_2O(\ell) \qquad \Delta H_2 = -286 \ kJ \ mol^{-1}$$

$$CH_4(g) + 2O_2(g) \rightarrow CO_2(g) + 2H_2O(\ell) \qquad \Delta H_3 = -891 \ kJ \ mol^{-1}$$

The equations can be arranged in the following energy cycle:

Top Tip

Enthalpies of combustion and formation can be found in the SQA data booklet.

Important notes on the energy cycle:

1. ΔH_2 has to be **multiplied by 2**, i.e. $2\Delta H_2$, because in the target equation 2 moles of hydrogen react.

2. ΔH_3 has to be **reversed**, i.e. $-\Delta H_3$, because in the cycle the carbon dioxide and water combine to form methane and oxygen, the reverse of combustion.

3. Applying Hess's law:

$$\Delta H_f = \Delta H_1 + 2\Delta H_2 - \Delta H_3$$
$$= -394 + (2 \times -286) - (-891)$$
ΔH_f = −75 kJ mol^{-1}

TOP TIP

It is not always necessary to draw out an energy cycle. By writing out the equation for route 1 (target equation) and the equations for the enthalpy of reaction for each of the steps in route 2, rearranging them as required, and then applying Hess's law, the enthalpy of reaction can be calculated.

Quick Test 40

1. The equation for the formation of ethene is $2C(s) + 2H_2(g) \rightarrow C_2H_4(g)$.

   Calculate the enthalpy of formation of ethene, using the enthalpies of combustion shown below:

   $$C(s) \quad + \quad O_2(g) \quad \rightarrow \quad CO_2(g) \qquad \qquad \Delta H_1 = -394 \text{ kJ mol}^{-1}$$
   $$H_2(g) \quad + \quad \tfrac{1}{2}O_2(g) \quad \rightarrow \quad H_2O(\ell) \qquad \qquad \Delta H_2 = -286 \text{ kJ mol}^{-1}$$
   $$C_2H_4(g) + \quad 3O_2(g) \quad \rightarrow \quad 2CO_2(g) + 2H_2O(\ell) \qquad \Delta H_3 = -1411 \text{ kJ mol}^{-1}$$

2. Calculate the enthalpy of formation of methanol from the enthalpy of combustion of carbon, hydrogen and methanol (use the SQA data booklet for enthalpies of combustion):

   $$C(s) + 2H_2(g) + \tfrac{1}{2}O_2 \rightarrow CH_3OH(\ell) \ \Delta H_f \text{ (target equation)}$$

Chemical energy 4

Bond and mean bond enthalpies

TOP TIP

Bond enthalpies and mean bond enthalpies can be found in the SQA data booklet.

Bond enthalpy is the energy required to break one mole of bonds between the atoms in a mole of gaseous diatomic molecules, at standard temperature and pressure (25°C and 1 atmosphere).

For diatomic molecules such as hydrogen (H_2) and hydrogen chloride (HCl) there is only one possible bond energy for each, as the H–H bond and H–Cl bond can only exist in these molecules.

This is not the case for the likes of the C–C bond, which can exist in alkanes, cycloalkanes, alcohols, etc. The C–C bond will have a slightly different bond enthalpy depending on the type of molecule it exists in. The bond enthalpy quoted in these cases is the **mean bond enthalpy**, which is an average value.

Bond breaking is an endothermic process, because energy has to be put in to overcome the force of attraction between the atoms.

Bond making is an exothermic process – if energy needs to be put in to break a bond, then the same amount of energy should be given out when the same bond forms.

Estimating enthalpy changes

Bond enthalpies and mean bond enthalpies can be used to estimate the enthalpy changes for different reactions. The enthalpy of reaction is the difference between the energy needed to break bonds and the energy released when bonds are made. When a fuel burns, for example, the energy produced when bonds are made is greater than the energy needed to break bonds between reactant molecules.

Example

Burning hydrogen in oxygen:

Bond breaking	Bond making

$$\text{H–H(g)} + \tfrac{1}{2}\text{O=O(g)} \quad \rightarrow \quad \text{H–O–H(g)}$$

$$436 \quad + \quad \tfrac{1}{2}(498) \qquad \qquad 2\,(-463)$$

$$\Delta H = 436 + 249 \qquad + \qquad (-926)$$

$$\Delta H = -241{\cdot}0 \text{ kJ mol}^{-1}$$

Example

Use bond enthalpies and mean bond enthalpies to estimate the energy released when 1 mole of methanol is burned.

$$CH_3OH(g) + \frac{3}{2}O_2(g) \rightarrow CO_2(g) + 2H_2O(g)$$

Worked answer:

Total endothermic change for bond breaking:	Total exothermic change for bond making:	Bond enthalpies in kJ mol^{-1}
$3 \times$ C–H	$2 \times$ C=O	C–H = 412
$1 \times$ C–O	$4 \times$ O–H	C–O = 360
$1 \times$ O–H	= $(2 \times -743) + (4 \times -463)$	O–H = 463
$1\frac{1}{2} \times$ O=O	= -3338 kJ	O=O = 498
= $(3 \times 412) + 360$		C=O = 743
$+ 463 + (1\frac{1}{2} \times 498)$		
= $+2806$ kJ		

$$\Delta H_c = +2806 - 3338 = -532 \text{ kJ mol}^{-1}$$

TOP TIP

Using this method gives an enthalpy of combustion which is regarded as an estimate and is different from the data booklet value. This is because not all of the reactants and products are gases in their standard states, and also the mean bond enthalpy values used are average values.

Quick Test 41

1. Use the bond enthalpies and mean bond enthalpies in the SQA data booklet to estimate the enthalpy of combustion of propane:

$$C_3H_8(g) + 5O_2(g) \rightarrow 3CO_2(g) + 4H_2O(g)$$

2. Use the bond enthalpies and mean bond enthalpies in the SQA data booklet to estimate the enthalpy of combustion of ethanol:

$$C_2H_5OH(g) + 3O_2(g) \rightarrow 2CO_2(g) + 3H_2O(g)$$

Equilibria 1

Reversible reactions and equilibrium

Many of the reactions we have looked at so far, such as neutralisation and combustion, appear to be irreversible and, for practical purposes, they are. Burning magnesium in oxygen can be considered as a reaction which goes to completion:

$$2Mg(s) + O_2(g) \rightarrow 2MgO(s)$$

The single arrow in the equation tells us the reaction is irreversible and goes to completion.

However, many reactions can be reversed. A **reversible reaction** is one which can take place in both directions, i.e. the products can re-form reactants.

A reversible reaction you are likely to have seen in the laboratory is the colour change which happens when water is added to blue cobalt chloride paper and it turns pink. The paper changes back to blue when the paper is warmed and the water is evaporated off.

Any general reversible reaction can be represented as:

$$A + B \rightleftharpoons C + D$$

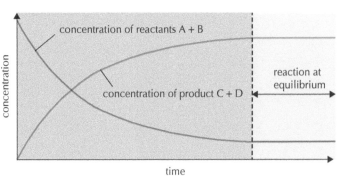

forward rate decreases as concentration decreases

rate of reaction

A + B   at equilibrium the rates of the forward and backward reactions are the same

C + D

reverse rate increases as concentration increases

time

The double arrow indicates the reaction is reversible. At the start: Concentrations of A and B are high, so the rate of forward reaction (left to right) is high.

Concentrations of C and D are zero, so the rate of backward reaction (right to left) is zero.

As the reaction progresses: Concentrations of A and B decrease, so the rate of forward reaction decreases.

Concentrations of C and D increase, so the rate of backward reaction increases.

This continues until the two rates are equal – a state of balance is formed. This is known as **dynamic equilibrium**. At this point the concentrations of reactants and products are unchanging, but seldom the same.

concentration

concentration of reactants A + B

concentration of product C + D

reaction at equilibrium

time

The changes in concentration of reactants and products and rate of the forward and backward reactions with time are shown in the graphs.

TOP TIP

An equilibrium can only be established where no reactants or products can escape – this is known as a **closed system**.

TOP TIP

The word 'dynamic' is used to indicate that although the concentrations of reactants and products are unchanging and it may appear that the reaction has stopped, at equilibrium the forward and backward reactions are still happening, but at the same rate.

The position of equilibrium

In some reactions equilibrium isn't reached until the forward reaction is nearly complete – we say the equilibrium lies to the right. The concentration of the products is greater than the concentration of the reactants. This is shown in the left-hand graph, for the general reaction $A + B \rightleftharpoons C + D$.

In other reactions, equilibrium can be reached early in the reaction – we say the equilibrium lies to the left. This is shown in the right-hand graph. The concentrations of C and D are much less than A and B so the equilibrium is to the left.

For a reversible reaction which forms an equilibrium, the same equilibrium position is reached regardless of whether we start from reactants or products.

Quick Test 42

1. A flask (flask 1) containing 0·5 mol of hydrogen and 0·5 mol of iodine, and another flask (flask 2) with 1 mol of hydrogen iodide, were placed in a water bath and kept at the same temperature. After 90 mins the concentration of hydrogen iodide in both flasks was found to be 0·78 mol.

   (a) Explain this result.

   (b) Write a balanced formula equation to summarise the reaction.

2. The graph shows how the concentration of reactants and products changes as an equilibrium is formed.

   (a) (i) Does the graph represent the change in concentration for an equilibrium which lies to the left or right?

   (ii) Explain your answer.

   (b) At which point on the graph is equilibrium reached?

Equilibria 2

Changing the position of equilibrium

Many industrial processes involve reactions which are reversible. This creates challenges for industrial chemists, who want to make as much product as possible, as economically as possible. They have to be able to change the reaction conditions so that the maximum amount of product is formed. Equilibrium is reached when the rates of the forward and backward reactions become equal, so the factors which affect the rate of a reaction might affect the equilibrium position.

TOP TIP

The position of the equilibrium of a system changes to minimise the effect of any imposed change in condition – concentration, pressure and temperature.

Changing concentration

The reaction between iron(III) ions (Fe^{3+}) and thiocyanate ions (CNS^-) can be used to show the effect on an equilibrium when the concentration of reactants or products is changed:

$$Fe^{3+}(aq) \ + \ CNS^-(aq) \ \rightleftharpoons \ [FeCNS]^{2+}(aq)$$

pale yellow   colourless   red

The two reactants are mixed and a deep red solution forms, which is diluted with water until it is an orange colour, and finally poured into four separate test tubes. Test tube A is kept as a control – nothing else is added to it. The other three solutions (B, C and D) each have chemicals added to them, which causes a colour change in each test tube, as shown in the diagram.

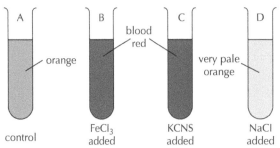

A — orange — control
B — blood red — FeCl$_3$ added
C — KCNS added
D — very pale orange — NaCl added

TOP TIP

Increasing the concentration of reactants shifts the equilibrium position right, i.e. more product is formed.
Reducing the concentration of reactants shifts the equilibrium position left, i.e. product re-forms reactants.
Removing product shifts the equilibrium position right, i.e. more product is formed.
Adding product shifts the equilibrium position left, i.e. more reactant is formed.

Observations:

Test tubes B and C: The concentration of one of the reactants is increased. The equilibrium position shifts to the right, forming more product. This is indicated by the blood-red colour forming as more $[FeCNS]^{2+}(aq)$ ions are made.

Test tube D: Adding NaCl removes $Fe^{3+}(aq)$ ions – the Cl^- ions form a complex with $Fe^{3+}(aq)$ ions. This results in the concentration of $Fe^{3+}(aq)$ ions decreasing so the equilibrium shifts left, forming more reactants. This is indicated by the orange solution becoming paler as the red $[FeCNS]^{2+}(aq)$ ions form $Fe^{3+}(aq)$ (pale yellow) and $CNS^-(aq)$ (colourless) ions.

Changing pressure

The effect of changing the pressure can be observed using nitrogen dioxide (NO_2), a brown gas. Nitrogen dioxide actually exists in equilibrium with dinitrogen tetroxide (N_2O_4), which is colourless.

$$N_2O_4(g) \quad \rightleftharpoons \quad 2NO_2(g)$$
colourless   brown

If the gas mixture is placed in a glass syringe, the effect of increasing and decreasing the pressure can be seen by noting the colour change in the gas.

More N_2O_4 formed – equilibrium shifts left in direction of fewer moles of molecules.

More NO_2 formed – equilibrium shifts right in direction of more moles of molecules.

TOP TIP

Increasing pressure causes an equilibrium to move towards where there are fewer moles of gas molecules.
Decreasing the pressure causes an equilibrium to move towards where there are more moles of gas molecules.
If an equilibrium has the same number of moles of gas on each side of the equation then changing the pressure will have no effect on the position of the equilibrium.
If an equilibrium has no gases then changing pressure will have no effect on the position of equilibrium.

Quick Test 43

1. Bromine dissolves in water to form the equilibrium shown in the following equation:
$$Br_2(\ell) + H_2O(\ell) \rightleftharpoons Br^-(aq) + BrO^-(aq) + 2H^+(aq)$$
   (a) Explain the effect on the equilibrium if dilute nitric acid (source of $H^+(aq)$ ions) is added.
   (b) Explain the effect on the equilibrium if dilute potassium hydroxide (source of OH^- (aq) ions) is added.

2. In the industrial preparation of methanol, a mixture of carbon monoxide and hydrogen gas (synthesis gas) is passed over a catalyst:
$$CO(g) + 2H_2(g) \rightleftharpoons CH_3OH(g)$$
   (a) (i) State the pressure conditions which would most likely be used to improve the amount of methanol.
   (ii) Justify your answer.
   (b) The methanol is liquefied and drained off as it forms. Explain why this increases the yield of methanol.

Equilibria 3

Changing temperature

The effect of temperature on an equilibrium depends on whether a reaction is exothermic or endothermic. If, for example, the forward reaction is exothermic, then the backward reaction will be endothermic. The effect of changing temperature can be shown using the nitrogen dioxide (NO_2), dinitrogen tetroxide (N_2O_4) equilibrium:

$$N_2O_4 \quad \rightleftharpoons \quad 2NO_2 \quad \Delta H = \text{positive}$$
$$\text{colourless} \qquad\quad \text{brown}$$

For an equation written this way, the ΔH value is for the forward reaction, which in this case is endothermic (positive). The enthalpy change for the backward reaction must therefore be exothermic (negative).

Three test tubes of the gas mixture are prepared so that they all have the same brown colour at room temperature. One is kept at room temperature (B), another (C) is placed in a beaker of hot water to raise the temperature and the third (A) is placed in a freezing ice/salt mixture to lower the temperature.

> ### Top Tip
>
> For a system in equilibrium, a rise in temperature favours the endothermic reaction. A decrease in temperature favours the exothermic reaction.

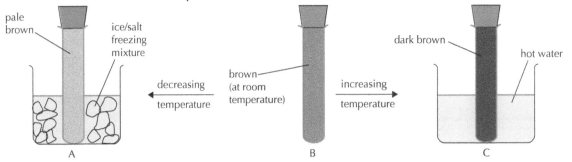

Observations:

Test tube C: The colour gradually darkens compared to (B), indicating that more NO_2 (brown) is formed. The equilibrium is moving right, the direction of the endothermic reaction.

Test tube A: The colour gradually lightens compared to (B), indicating that more N_2O_4 (colourless) is formed. The equilibrium is moving left, the direction of the exothermic reaction.

Adding a catalyst

A catalyst speeds up a reaction because it gives a different route to products which overall has a lower activation energy (E_a) than the reaction would have without a catalyst. This is shown in the potential energy diagram below.

The potential energy diagram above shows that a catalyst lowers the energy of activation not only for the forward reaction, but also for the backward reaction. This means that in a reversible reaction, the rate of the backward reaction will also be increased. This means that the catalyst does not affect the equilibrium position – it does, however, allow the equilibrium position to be reached more quickly. Catalysts also allow reactions to be carried out at lower temperatures, which makes the reactions more economical.

> **TOP TIP**
>
> Catalysts are an essential in the economical production of chemicals on an industrial scale, many of which are produced by routes that involve reactions which are reversible.

> **TOP TIP**
>
> If a system at equilibrium is subjected to a change, the system will adjust to oppose the effect of the change.

Quick Test 44

1. In the industrial manufacture of methanol, the mixture of carbon monoxide and hydrogen gas (synthesis gas) used can be produced from methane:

    $$CH_4(g) + H_2O(g) \rightleftharpoons CO(g) + 3H_2(g) \quad \Delta H = +206 \text{ kJ mol}^{-1}$$

    (a) Predict the effect increasing the temperature would have on the yield of synthesis gas.

    (b) Explain the reasoning behind your answer.

2. (a) Predict the effect increasing the temperature would have on the following equilibrium:

    $$4NH_3(g) + 5O_2(g) \rightleftharpoons 4NO(g) + 6H_2O(\ell) \quad \Delta H = -908 \text{ kJ mol}^{-1}$$

    (b) Explain the reasoning behind your answer.

3. (a) Explain why the addition of a catalyst to a reversible reaction has no effect on the position of the equilibrium, even though it provides a route from reactants to products which has a lower activation energy.

    (b) What effect does the addition of a catalyst have on a chemical equilibrium?

Equilibria 4

Equilibria in industry

The Haber process is the industrial manufacture of ammonia from nitrogen and hydrogen:

$$N_2(g) + 3H_2(g) \rightleftharpoons 2NH_3(g) \quad \Delta H = -92 \text{ kJ mol}^{-1}$$

This is a reversible reaction, which in a closed system would form a dynamic equilibrium and, thus, the equilibrium position can be changed by altering certain conditions.

1. Pressure

There are four moles of gases on the left-hand side and two moles on the right-hand side. Increasing the pressure would cause the equilibrium to shift to the right because there are fewer moles of gas on the right, i.e. more ammonia would be formed.

2. Temperature

The forward reaction is exothermic, so a drop in temperature would cause the equilibrium to shift to the right.

In industry, however, the conditions used are not always the theoretical conditions, mainly for economic reasons. In choosing the right temperature, manufacturers must consider the percentage yield and rate of reaction. Temperature has a major effect on the rate of reaction. If the temperature is too low, which would in theory result in more ammonia being formed, the rate at which ammonia is formed would not be fast enough. Manufacturers use a combination of a moderate temperature and a catalyst to ensure the rate of production of ammonia is high.

High pressure improves the yield and rate of formation, but the higher the pressure, the more it costs to build and run the plant. The higher the pressure, the thicker the pipes need to be, and the more energy is needed.

The graph shows how the percentage of ammonia in the equilibrium mixture varies at different pressures and temperatures.

Most manufacturers use:

- a relatively high pressure of between 100 and 200 atmospheres
- a moderate temperature of around 400°C
- a finely divided iron catalyst.

The operating conditions are not a closed system. The ammonia is continually removed so equilibrium is not reached, and the reactants are recycled and continuously passed over the catalyst. This improves the yield of ammonia by up to 98%. Researchers are continuing to search for alternative catalysts which will work at lower temperature and pressure, reducing costs.

In the USA scientists are working on alternative sources of hydrogen. The current source of hydrogen is mainly natural gas, which is a finite resource. Researchers are using electricity produced from wind power to electrolyse water and produce hydrogen.

The diagram opposite summarises the effect of increasing temperature and pressure in the Haber process.

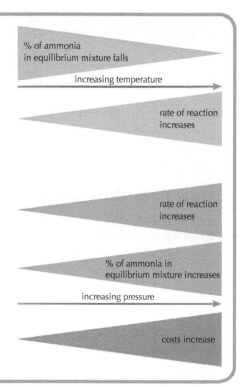

Quick Test 45

The flow diagram summarises the ammonia manufacturing process.

1. In the steam-reforming stage, hydrogen is made by reacting methane and steam at 850°C and 30 atmospheres pressure:

$$CH_4(g) + H_2O(g) \rightleftharpoons CO(g) + 3H_2(g) \qquad \Delta H = +210 \text{ kJ mol}^{-1}$$

(a) Explain why a high temperature is used.

(b) Suggest why a high pressure is used, even though the equation indicates a low pressure should be used.

2. Ammonia is formed in the synthesis reaction vessel.

(a) Explain why the iron catalyst is finely divided.

(b) What is the effect of reducing the concentration of ammonia in the equilibrium mixture by removing it in the ammonia condenser?

(c) Suggest why the N_2:H_2 mixture is in a 1:3 ratio as it enters the synthesis reaction vessel.

Chemical analysis 1

Chromatography

Chromatography is a technique which can be used to separate, identify and in some instances obtain individual substances from complex mixtures. There are many different chromatographic methods, including paper, thin layer, gas and gas-liquid.

How does chromatography work?

The principles for each type of chromatography are the same. The differences in **size** and **polarity** of molecules are used to separate them. A liquid or gas (the **mobile phase**) carries the molecules of a substance over or through a solid or a liquid absorbed onto a solid (the **stationary phase**).

Two methods commonly used in a school laboratory are **paper chromatography** and **thin layer chromatography** (TLC).

In paper chromatography, water on the surface of the paper acts as the stationary phase. In TLC, glass plates are coated with silica gel or alumina, which have very polar hydroxyl groups on their surface, and act as the stationary phase. Spots of the mixture are put onto the paper or plate, and they are placed in a suitable solvent – the mobile phase.

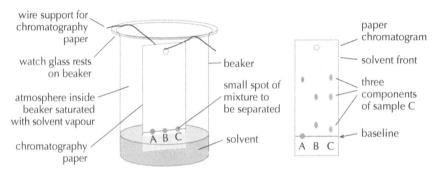

As the solvent begins to move up the paper or TLC plate, it dissolves the compounds that have been spotted on the chromatogram. The compounds will then move up the chromatogram as the solvent moves upwards. Molecules continually change from being in the mobile phase, i.e. dissolved in the solvent and moving, to being stopped due to intermolecular attractions with the molecules of the stationary phase.

TOP TIP

The speed at which the compounds move depends on two factors:
- how attracted they are to the stationary phase
- their solubility in the mobile phase (the solvent).

Identifying what's in a mixture

Components of mixtures separated by paper or thin layer chromatography can sometimes be observed because they are coloured, e.g. the inks in felt-tip pens. More often they have to be developed in some way. The diagram on page 117 shows how two amino acids can be separated and then identified.

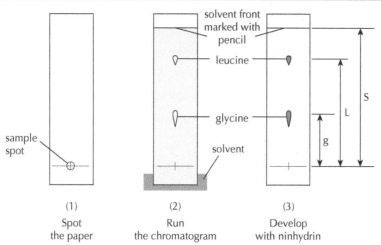

(1)   (2)   (3)

Spot   Run   Develop

the paper   the chromatogram   with ninhydrin

Separating and identifying the amino acids leucine and glycine in a sample.
Amino acids are colourless and become visible when sprayed with ninhydrin.

Components of a mixture can also be identified by the distance they travel compared to the distance travelled by the solvent – the **solvent front**. This is called the R_f **value** (the retention or retardation factor). The R_f value is constant for a particular substance if other conditions such as paper and solvent used remain the same.

Calculating the R_f value

$$R_f = \frac{\text{distance travelled by compound}}{\text{distance travelled by solvent}}$$

For the chromatogram above, the R_f value for leucine is:

$$R_f = \frac{L}{S}$$

$$= \frac{3 \cdot 5}{4 \cdot 5}$$

$$R_f = 0 \cdot 78$$

> ### TOP TIP
>
> R_f values have no units. Different compounds have different R_f values.
> For molecules with similar polarity the larger the molecule, the smaller the R_f value, i.e. the slower it will move up the plate or paper.
> A polar molecule will have a higher R_f value in polar solvents than it will have if a non-polar solvent is used.

Quick Test 46

1. Two compounds, A and B, are to be separated using paper chromatography. A is very soluble in the mobile phase and almost insoluble in the stationary phase. B has greater solubility in the stationary phase than in the mobile phase.

   (a) Which will travel further during chromatography?

   (b) Explain your answer to (a).

2. (a) Suggest why, in the chromatogram on page 116, one of the components in mixture A has not moved off the baseline.

   (b) Two of the mixtures in the chromatogram on page 116 contain one component which is the same. State which two and explain how you reached your conclusion.

3. (a) Calculate the R_f value for glycene in the chromatogram above if it travels 1·7 cm from the baseline.

   (b) Explain why R_f values can be used to identify a component in a mixture.

Chemical analysis 2

Using chromatography in analysis

Chromatography is used in laboratories to aid chemical analysis in many different situations.

Area	Use
Pharmaceutical companies	Determines amount of each chemical found in new product.
Hospitals	Detects chemicals in a patient's blood stream.
Law enforcement	Compares a sample found at a crime scene to samples from suspects.
Environmental agencies	Determines the level of pollutants in the water supply.
Manufacturing	Follows the progress of a reaction and purifies a chemical needed to make other products such as medicines.

Paper chromatography

One use of paper chromatography is to separate and identify amino acids in a mixture.

Sometimes the amino acids in a mixture are not separated completely because they have similar solubilities in a particular solvent. To overcome this problem the paper is rotated through 90° and a different solvent is used to ensure a separation. This is known as two-way separation.

1. The mixture and known amino acids are spotted on the paper. The baseline is drawn using pencil, as ink is likely to separate out with the solvent.

2. As the solvent moves up the paper the amino acids move with it and separate out. At this stage the amino acids are invisible.

3. When the solvent front reaches the top of the paper, the paper is removed, dried and sprayed with ninhydrin to show up the amino acids as purple spots.

4. If the separation is not good enough the experiment is repeated and a two-way chromatogram is run.

Two-way paper chromatography can be used to improve the separation of components of a mixture. The green components in the first chromatogram are separated out in the second and appear as yellow and blue (colours are used here to make the separation clearer to see).

Thin layer chromatography (TLC)

The process of separation is similar to paper chromatography. However, TLC has the advantage of being faster and gives better separation. There are also several choices of the stationary phase, such as alumina and silica, and it is relatively cheap. TLC can be used in forensic science to identify explosive residues and to detect cannabis. The separated components can be retrieved by scraping off the spots on the stationary phase and dissolving them in a suitable solvent.

Gas chromatography (GC) and gas-liquid chromatography (GLC)

Gas chromatography (GC) and gas-liquid chromatography (GLC) are techniques which can separate mixtures of gases and volatile liquids. These techniques can be used to separate very small quantities. GLC has become a standard method for detecting banned substances in sport, and for accurately determining the amount of alcohol in a motorist's blood when it is near the legal limit.

A gas-liquid chromatogram is usually a graph with peaks appearing at different times depending on the retention time of each component in a sample. The graphs can be compared to the graph obtained for known samples. The graph opposite shows the contents of a soft drink. The four peaks indicate that four substances are present. The retention time of each substance is shown along the x-axis and the quantity of each substance is shown by the area under each peak (y-axis).

TOP TIP

The amount of substance present can be calculated from the area under each peak, not from the height of the peak. This is usually automatically calculated by a computer connected to the machine.

Quick Test 47

1. (a) Suggest why, when drawing the baseline on chromatography paper or a TLC plate, pencil is used.

    (b) Suggest why, when using two-way chromatography, two different mobile solvents are used.

2. (a) A database of retention times is kept for each GLC machine for known compounds. Suggest why it is essential to keep the conditions in the machine constant after forming the database.

    (b) By inspection of the chromatogram above, estimate which of the components there is most of and explain how you came to your conclusion.

Chemical analysis 3

Volumetric analysis

Volumetric analysis involves using a solution of accurately known concentration to determine the concentration of another substance. In order to do this, the concentration of the substance being used to react with the compound needs to be known accurately.

A solution of accurately known concentration is referred to as a **standard solution**.

Preparing a standard solution

Suppose you wish to prepare 500 cm³ of a 0·10 mol l⁻¹ sodium carbonate solution.

Step 1: Calculate the **mass** of sodium carbonate required, from the number of moles.

$$\text{No. of moles (n)} = \text{concentration (c)} \times \text{volume (V)}$$
$$= 0·5 \times 0·1$$
$$= 0·05 \text{ mol}$$

$$\text{Mass required (m)} = \text{moles (n)} \times \text{gram formula mass (GFM)}$$
$$= 0·05 \times 106$$
$$= 5·30 \text{ g}$$

Step 2: Weigh out accurately the required mass and dissolve it in deionised water in a small beaker.

Step 3: Pour the solution into a volumetric flask and rinse all of the solution out of the beaker using a water bottle.

Step 4: More deionised water is added until it reaches the etched line on the neck of the flask. The flask is stoppered and then inverted, to ensure the solution is fully mixed.

deionised water bottle

bottom of meniscus sits on etched line

volumetric flask

The concentration of the standard solution can be calculated if the exact mass weighed out is known – although the mass has to be measured accurately, it doesn't need to be exactly 5·30 g. Let's say 5·39 g was actually weighed out:

$$n = \frac{m}{GFM} = \frac{5·39}{106} = 0·051 \text{ mol}$$
$$c = \frac{n}{V} = \frac{0·051}{0·50} = 0·102 \text{ mol l}^{-1}$$

This standard solution is used in the calculation of the concentration of an acid in the example in **(1) Acid-base titration** below.

Calculating an unknown concentration

(1) Acid-base titration

The standard solution prepared above can be used in a titration, the results of which can be used to calculate the concentration of another solution using the following relationship:

$$\frac{(\text{concentration} \times \text{volume})_{\text{alkali}}}{\text{balancing no.}_{\text{alkali}}} = \frac{(\text{concentration} \times \text{volume})_{\text{acid}}}{\text{balancing no.}_{\text{acid}}}$$

Example

19·7 cm³ of 0·102 mol l⁻¹ sodium carbonate solution was required to neutralise 25·0 cm³ of dilute hydrochloric acid solution.
Find the concentration of the hydrochloric acid.

TOP TIP

You don't have to memorise the relationship between volume, concentration and balancing numbers – it is given in the SQA data booklet as: $\dfrac{c_1 V_1}{n_1} = \dfrac{c_2 V_2}{n_2}$

$$Na_2CO_3(aq) \;+\; 2HCl(aq) \;\rightarrow\; 2NaCl(aq) \;+\; CO_2(g) \;+\; H_2O(\ell)$$

Worked answer:

The balancing number for sodium carbonate is 1 and for hydrochloric acid is 2.

$$\frac{(\text{volume} \times \text{concentration})_{\text{acid}}}{\text{balancing no.}_{\text{acid}}} = \frac{(\text{volume} \times \text{concentration})_{\text{alkali}}}{\text{balancing no.}_{\text{alkali}}}$$

$$\frac{25 \cdot 0 \times \text{conc}}{2} = \frac{19 \cdot 7 \times 0 \cdot 102}{1}$$

$$12 \cdot 5 \times \text{conc} = 2 \cdot 01$$

$$\text{conc} = \frac{2 \cdot 58}{12 \cdot 5}$$

$$\text{conc} = 0 \cdot 161 \text{ mol l}^{-1}$$

TOP TIP

In an acid/base titration a coloured indicator is normally used to show when the end-point is reached. Titres within 0·2 cm³ are considered **concordant**.

TOP TIP

You don't have to change volumes to litres because volume appears on both sides of the relationship.

(2) Redox titration

Volumetric analysis can be applied to a redox reaction. For example, the concentration of a solution of a reducing agent can be found using an oxidising agent.

Example

The concentration of iron(II) ions (reducing agent) in a solution can be found by titrating 20 cm³ portions of the solution with acidified potassium permanganate solution (oxidising agent) with a concentration of 0·101 mol l⁻¹.
The average titre was 13·7 cm³.

Oxidation	$Fe^{2+} \rightarrow Fe^{3+}(aq) + e^-$
Reduction	$MnO_4^-(aq) + 8H^+(aq) + 5e^- \rightarrow Mn^{2+}(aq) + 4H_2O(\ell)$
Redox	$MnO_4^-(aq) + 8H^+(aq) + 5Fe^{2+}(aq) \rightarrow Mn^{2+}(aq) + 8H_2O(\ell) + 5Fe^{3+}(aq)$

Worked answer:

$$\frac{(concentration \times volume)_{reducing\ agent}}{balancing\ no._{reducing\ agent}} = \frac{(concentration \times volume)_{oxidising\ agent}}{balancing\ no._{oxidising\ agent}}$$

$$\frac{20 \cdot 0 \times conc\ Fe^{2+}}{5} = \frac{13 \cdot 7 \times 0 \cdot 101}{1}$$

$4 \times conc\ Fe^{2+} = 1 \cdot 384$

$conc\ Fe^{2+} = \dfrac{1 \cdot 384}{4}$

$conc\ Fe^{2+} = 0 \cdot 346\ mol\ l^{-1}$

TOP TIP

The balancing numbers are obtained from the redox equation. The oxidation equation has to be multiplied by 5 to balance the number of electrons in the reduction and oxidation equations.

In the reaction in the worked example the acidified permanganate acts as its own indicator. As the purple permanganate solution is added the permanganate ions are reduced by the Fe^{2+} ions to colourless Mn^{2+} ions. At the end-point when all of the Fe^{2+} ions have reacted the solution will be purple.

TOP TIP

Acidified potassium dichromate (orange) can also be used a self-indicator for redox titrations.

The volume of a particular reactant needed to react completely in a redox reaction can be calculated.

Example

Calculate the volume of acidified $0 \cdot 11\ mol\ l^{-1}$ potassium permanganate ($KMnO_4$) needed to completely oxidise 25 cm^3 of $0 \cdot 16\ mol\ l^{-1}$ hydrogen peroxide solution (H_2O_2).

$$2MnO_4^-(aq) + 6H^+(aq) + 5H_2O_2(\ell) \rightarrow 2Mn^{2+}(aq) + 8H_2O(\ell) + 5O_2(g)$$

Worked answer:

$$\frac{(concentration \times volume)_{potassium\ permanganate}}{balancing\ no._{potassium\ permanganate}} = \frac{(concentration \times volume)_{hydrogen\ peroxide}}{balancing\ no._{hydrogen\ peroxide}}$$

$$\frac{0 \cdot 11 \times vol\ KMnO_4}{2} = \frac{0 \cdot 16 \times 25}{5}$$

$$vol\ KMnO_4 = \frac{0 \cdot 16 \times 25 \times 2}{5 \times 0 \cdot 11}$$

$$vol\ KMnO_4 = 15 \cdot 5\ cm^3$$

The mass of a substance dissolved in a solution can be calculated.

Example

A vitamin C tablet was dissolved in some deionised water and made up to 250 cm³ in a standard flask. 25 cm³ of the solution was titrated with 0·029 mol l⁻¹ iodine solution. The average titre was 17·5 cm³.

Calculate the mass of vitamin C ($C_6H_8O_6$) in the tablet.

$$C_6H_8O_6 + I_2 \rightarrow 2I^- + C_6H_6O_6 + 2H^+$$

Worked answer:

Step 1: From the balanced equation, 1 mole of vitamin C reacts with 1 mole of iodine.

Calculate the number of moles of iodine from the information given. The number of moles of vitamin C reacting will be the same.

Moles of iodine (n) = c × V

$$= 0·029 \times 0·0175$$

$$= 0·00051 \text{ mol } (5·1 \times 10^{-4} \text{ mol})$$

This is the number of moles in the 25 cm³ in the sample titrated.

The tablet was dissolved in 250 cm³ of water so the number of moles of vitamin C will be 10 times this value, i.e. 0·0051 moles ($5·1 \times 10^{-3}$ mol).

Step 2: Calculate the gram formula mass (GFM) of the vitamin C and multiply it by the number of moles (n, found in step 1) to get the mass of vitamin C.

GFM of vitamin C ($C_6H_8O_6$) = 176 g

Mass (m) of vitamin C in tablet = n × GFM

$$= 0·0051 \times 176$$

$$= 0·898 \text{ g}$$

Quick Test 48

1. (a) Calculate the mass of sodium hydroxide required to make 500 cm³ of a standard solution with a concentration of 0·01 mol l⁻¹.

   (b) Describe how you would prepare the standard solution in part (a).

2. A 25 cm³ solution of sulfuric acid was titrated with a standard sodium hydroxide solution with a concentration of 0·109 mol l⁻¹. The average titre was 17·8 cm³. Calculate the concentration of the sulfuric acid.

   $$2NaOH(aq) + H_2SO_4(aq) \rightarrow Na_2SO_4(aq) + 2H_2O(\ell)$$

3. Calculate the concentration of a hydrogen peroxide solution (H_2O_2) if 25 cm³ of the solution reacts completely with 14·8 cm³ of acidified potassium permanganate solution with a concentration of 0·11 mol l⁻¹.

   $$2MnO_4^-(aq) + 6H^+(aq) + 5H_2O_2(\ell) \rightarrow 2Mn^{2+}(aq) + 8H_2O(\ell) + 5O_2(g)$$

Learning checklist

Getting the most from reactants

In this section you have learned:

- When making new products, industrial chemists have to consider the most economical way to make them in order to maximise profit and minimise the effect on the environment.
- Factors influencing industrial process design include:
  - availability, sustainability and cost of feedstocks
  - product yield
  - marketability of by-products
  - recyclability of reactants and solvents
  - energy requirements
- Environmental considerations include:
  - waste prevention
  - safer product design and products
  - use of renewable feedstocks
  - designing products that will biodegrade.
- The percentage yield is a way of measuring the efficiency of a chemical process:

$$\text{percentage yield (\%)} = \frac{\text{actual yield}}{\text{theoretical yield}} \times 100$$

- The atom economy is a way to measure the efficiency of a reaction:

$$\text{atom economy (\%)} = \frac{\text{mass of desired product}}{\text{total mass of reactants}} \times 100$$

- Percentage yield and atom economy have to be considered together when deciding the efficiency of a process.
- If the cost of feedstocks and the percentage yield are known for a reaction, then the cost of the reactants can be calculated.
- The mole ratio of atoms/ionic units in a compound can be worked out from a chemical formula.
- The mole ratio of reactants and products can be worked out from a balanced equation.
- The mass of one mole of any substance, in grams (g), is equal to the gram formula mass (GFM) and can be calculated using relative atomic masses.
- Masses/moles reacting and produced can be calculated from mole ratios in balanced equations.
- If the cost of feedstocks and the percentage yield are known for a reaction, then the cost of the reactants can be calculated.
- Masses, moles, concentrations and volumes of solutions reacting and being produced can be calculated from mole ratios in balanced equations.
- Reactants in excess and the limiting reactant can be calculated using the mole ratios in balanced equations.

- In order to ensure a costly reactant is converted to product an excess of the less expensive reactant(s) can be used.
- One mole of any gas occupies the same volume when measured at the same temperature and pressure, and is known as molar volume (V_m).
- Molar volume is measured in litres mol^{-1}.
- The volume of a gas can be calculated from the mass/number of moles and vice versa, given the molar volume.
- Volumes of reactant and product gases can be worked out from mole ratios in the balanced equation.

Controlling the rate of reaction

In this section you have learned:

- If the rate of an industrial reaction is too slow then the process will not be economically viable; if it is too fast then there is a risk of explosion.
- For reactants to form products they must first come in contact with each other (collide).
- The higher the concentration or pressure, the more collisions, and so the faster the reaction.
- The smaller the particle size, the bigger the surface area so the higher the chance of collision.
- Before collisions can be successful and lead to products, a minimum amount of energy, known as the activation energy (E_a), is required.
- Temperature is a measure of the average kinetic energy of the particles in a substance.
- Increasing the temperature increases the number of particles with energy equal to or greater than E_a. This results in more successful collisions and an increase in rate.
- Energy distribution diagrams can be drawn to show how increasing the temperature results in more particles with energy equal to or greater than E_a.
- Relative rate of reaction is inversely proportional to time, i.e. rate = 1/t.
- Rate of reaction is directly proportional to the concentration of the reactants.
- Rate of reaction is not directly proportional to temperature – a small increase in temperature results in a large increase in rate.
- Collision geometry has an effect on reaction rate.
- A potential energy diagram can be used to show the energy pathway for a reaction.
- Enthalpy is the name given to stored energy in chemicals and is given the symbol H.
- The enthalpy change is the energy difference between products and reactants.
- ΔH is the change in enthalpy for a reaction, and is measured in kJ or kJ mol^{-1} when one mole of substance is reacted or produced.
- ΔH and E_a can be calculated from a potential energy diagram for exothermic and endothermic reactions.
- ΔH values are negative for exothermic reactions and positive for endothermic reactions.

- E_a is the minimum amount of energy needed by colliding particles to form an activated complex.
- E_a is shown as an energy barrier in a potential energy diagram.
- An activated complex is an unstable arrangement of atoms formed at the top of the potential energy barrier.
- Catalysts provide an alternative pathway for reactants to form products – each step has a lower E_a than the uncatalysed reaction.
- A potential energy diagram can be used to show the effect of a catalyst on E_a.

Chemical energy

In this section you have learned:

- Enthalpy is a measure of the chemical energy of a substance.
- In industry, endothermic reactions require heat to be supplied, which incurs costs.
- In industry, the heat produced during exothermic reactions often needs to be removed to avoid the temperature rising too high.
- The enthalpy change associated with a reaction can be calculated from the quantity of heat energy released.
- The enthalpy of combustion is the enthalpy change when one mole of a substance burns completely in oxygen.
- Enthalpy of combustion is always exothermic.
- The quantity of heat energy released can be determined experimentally and calculated using $E_h = c \times m \times \Delta T$, where m = mass of water (kg); c = specific heat capacity of water (4.18 kJ kg^{-1} °C^{-1}); ΔT = change in temperature.
- Enthalpy of reaction is measured in kJ mol^{-1}.
- The quantities c, m and ΔT can be calculated from $E_h = cm\,\Delta T$.
- How to use Hess's law to calculate enthalpy changes.
- For a diatomic molecule, XY, the molar bond enthalpy is the energy required to break one mole of XY bonds.
- The mean molar bond enthalpy is the average bond enthalpy for bonds that exist in different molecular environments.
- The difference between the energy needed to break bonds in gaseous reactants and the energy released when new bonds are made gives an estimate of the enthalpy change for the reaction.

Equilibria

In this section you have learned:

- Many reactions are reversible.
- Reversible reactions attain a state of dynamic equilibrium when the rates of the forward and backward reactions are equal.
- Dynamic equilibrium will only be attained in a closed system where no products can escape, or reactants be added.
- At equilibrium the concentration of reactants and products remains constant, but rarely equal.
- Increasing the concentrations of reactants shifts the equilibrium to the right (products).
- Increasing the pressure shifts the equilibrium in the direction which results in a decrease in the number of moles of gas reactant or product.
- Increasing the temperature shifts the equilibrium in the direction of the endothermic reaction (ΔH = positive).
- Catalysts do not shift the equilibrium position, but allow equilibrium to be reached quicker.
- In industry, reaction conditions are changed so that product yield is maximised at the lowest cost.
- In industrial reactions, a balance has to be reached between shifting the equilibrium position towards products, and reaching the equilibrium position as quickly as possible.

Chemical analysis

In this section you have learned:

- There is a range of chromatography techniques, including paper, thin layer, gas and gas-liquid chromatography.
- Size and polarity of molecules are important factors in separating substances by chromatography.
- R_f values can be calculated.
- Volumetric analysis is a quantitative analysis technique.
- A standard solution is a solution of accurately known concentration.
- Volumetric analysis uses an accurately known concentration of one substance to find the concentration of another.
- Volumetric analysis includes the use of acid/base titrations and redox titrations.
- The end-point of a titration is the point where the reaction has just reached completion.
- Titre volumes within 0.2 cm^3 are considered concordant.
- An indicator is a substance that changes colour at the end-point of a reaction.
- In redox reactions some substances, e.g. potassium permanganate and potassium dichromate, can act as self-indicators.
- Given a balanced equation for the reaction occurring in any titration, the concentration or volume of one reactant can be calculated.

Researching chemistry 1

Skills of scientific inquiry

The purpose of the **Researching chemistry** area is to help you develop the skills of scientific inquiry – skills that are necessary to enable you to carry out chemical research. These skills will help you undertake the assignment that is part of the course assessment required by the SQA.

> **TOP TIP**
>
> The skills of scientific enquiry include:
> - **researching current literature** to help you understand the underlying chemistry of a topic
> - carrying out **practical investigative work** associated with the topic
> - **communicating your findings** clearly to others.

Sourcing information

No longer do we need to rely only on books for information. The internet has become the number one resource when seeking information on any subject. The world wide web holds a vast bank of instantly available information on every topic you can think of.

Text books and scientific journals are very useful sources of information. However, the internet has become an essential resource when seeking information on any subject. Following some simple rules will help ensure that the information you find when surfing the internet for information is relevant and reliable.

- Bookmark sites that you might want to return to for information.
- Check the URL suffix. Generally, government and academic sites give **reliable** information. Commercial sites and non-profit organisation sites may well give factually correct information but may be written for a particular purpose.
  - .ac.uk   UK academic institution
  - .edu   US academic institution
  - .gov.uk   UK government
  - .org.uk   UK non-profit organisation
  - .co.uk   UK company or individual
  - .com   multinational company
- Evaluate the information.

> **TOP TIP**
>
> It is important to consider whether or not the information you find is relevant and reliable. Is it supported by information on other websites? Does the information appear biased in any way?

Common laboratory apparatus you should be familiar with

In order to carry out the practical investigative work you will need to be familiar with, and know when and how to use, the pieces of chemical apparatus listed in the table.

beaker	distillation flask	measuring cylinder
burette	dropper	pipette and safety filler
condenser	evaporating basin	test tubes / boiling tubes
conical flask	filter funnel	thermometers
delivery tubes	filter paper	volumetric flasks

Techniques you should be familiar with

Filtration

Filtration is used to separate a solid residue from a liquid or solution.

Filtration

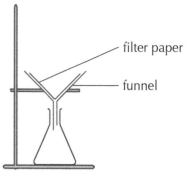

filter paper

funnel

Distillation

Distillation is used to separate a mixture of liquids – the liquid with the lower boiling point boils off first. A solvent can also be separated from a solution, collecting the solvent for reuse and leaving the solute in the distillation flask.

Distillation

thermometer

water out

condenser

water in

distillation flask   heat   anti-bump granules

Using a balance

In most instances it is sufficient to use a **top-pan balance** and use the 'tare' facility when weighing out chemicals. The tare button will re-set the balance to zero, allowing the mass being weighed to be read directly from the display.

Weighing by difference

Weighing by difference is considered to be the most accurate way of measuring the mass of a solid. A container plus the solid is weighed. Some of the solid is removed. The container and the remaining solid is reweighed. The difference in mass is the mass of the solid removed.

Collecting a gas

If the gas is insoluble in water then it can be collected by the **displacement of water**.

TOP TIP

One of the most effective ways of communicating experimental information is to use a well-drawn and labelled diagram. In chemistry, experimental set-ups are often represented by two-dimensional cross-sectional diagrams, known as line or sectional diagrams, like those shown on these pages.

measuring cylinder

dilute hydrochloric acid

marble chips

If a gas is soluble in water or the, volume of gas needs to be measured accurately, then a gas syringe can be used.

gas syringe

dilute hydrochloric acid

marble chips

Passing a gas through a liquid.

gas →

tube must be
above liquid

tube must be
in liquid

Often a gas is passed through a liquid as part of the separation process and through a solid, such as a drying agent, to remove water before it is collected. You may be asked to draw a diagram to show how both techniques could be carried out, and there are important points to note as highlighted in the diagrams.

Passing a gas through a drying agent.

drying agent must touch
top and bottom of tube.

Safe methods for heating

There are three common methods used in school chemistry laboratories for heating substances:

- **Bunsen burner**
- **water bath**
- **heating mantle**.

Using a Bunsen burner will heat something rapidly; care needs to be taken, particularly if flammable liquids are involved.

It is often better to use a water bath or heating mantle when heating flammable liquids.

Quick Test 49

1. Barium sulfate can be produced by the following reaction:

    $$BaCl_2(aq) + CuSO_4(aq) \rightarrow BaSO_4(s) + CuCl_2(aq)$$

    Suggest the most suitable method for obtaining a sample of the barium sulfate.

2. Ammonia is a very soluble gas, which can be produced in the laboratory by heating an ammonium salt with a base. Describe how you would collect a sample of the gas in the laboratory.

Researching chemistry 2

Titration

To carry out a **titration** accurately it is important to know how to use a pipette and burette properly.

Using a pipette

A **pipette** is used to deliver a precise volume of liquid. The pipette should be rinsed with water and then a small volume of the liquid to be pipetted. The liquid is then drawn up into the pipette, to above the graduation mark on the stem. It is then removed from the liquid, and the liquid in the pipette is slowly released, until the bottom of the meniscus just touches the graduation mark.

> **TOP TIP**
>
> Although the word 'liquid' is often used in a description, it can also be used to mean 'solution'.

> **TOP TIP**
>
> A safety filler should always be used to fill a pipette as shown in the photo opposite.

Using a burette

A **burette** is used to gradually and accurately add small volumes of solution to a reaction vessel, normally a conical flask. The burette should be rinsed with the liquid to be used and then clamped vertically in a burette stand.

The burette is filled to above the scale and then the tap opened to allow the liquid or solution to run down onto the scale. You must be careful to ensure that no air bubbles are trapped in the jet of the burette. The bottom of the meniscus is used to read the initial volume from the scale. It is important that your eye level is the same as the liquid level.

> **TOP TIP**
>
> A filter funnel can be used when filling a burette, but this must be removed before taking the initial burette reading and carrying out the titration.

Carrying out a titration

The correct procedure for carrying out a titration is to swirl the titration flask at the same time as adding the liquid from the burette. The stopcock of the burette is operated using the left hand if you are right-handed, and the flask swirled with the right hand. This can be difficult and requires practice. A white tile is used to help identify the permanent colour change that indicates the end-point of the titration.

> **TOP TIP**
>
> As the end-point is approached the liquid from the burette is added dropwise.

Analysis of data

Numerical results from experiments often need to be processed in some way. The data must be meaningful and correct. The table opposite gives some results from titrations carried out by a group of students.

Titration 2 is a 'rogue' result, i.e. it is way out compared to the others, perhaps because the student has made a mistake with the volumes of the other reactant used.

Titrations 3 and 4 are concordant – they are within 0·2 cm³ of each other and can be used to calculate the average titre. These results are said to be reproducible.

Titration	Volume (cm³)
1	19·8
2	26·3
3	17·7
4	17·9

TOP TIP

You should be able to calculate averages, eliminate rogue data and draw lines/curves of best fit.

Reproducibility

For an experiment to be classed as reproducible it has to provide the same results, within experimental error, when repeated. The table opposite gives some results for a titration which are not reproducible because none of the results are close enough to each other.

Titration	Volume (cm³)
1	18·8
2	22·3
3	15·7
4	17·6

Measuring uncertainty

Uncertainty is a measurement of the experimenter's best estimate of how far an experimental quantity might be from the 'true value'. For example, a measurement of 5·07 g +/− 0·02 g means the actual value might lie between 5·05 g and 5·09 g.

Quick Test 50

1. Calculate the average titre that should be used in a calculation from the results in the table at the top of the page.

2. The alcohol content of wine was analysed by four students. Each student carried out the experiment three times.

	Experiment 1 (%)	Experiment 2 (%)	Experiment 3 (%)
Student A	10·0	9·0	8·0
Student B	6·4	6·5	6·5
Student C	6·5	6·7	6·9
Student D	9·0	8·5	9·6

Which student obtained the most reproducible results?

Glossary

ΔH: see **enthalpy change**.

ΔH_c: see **standard enthalpy of combustion**.

ΔH_f: see **standard enthalpy of formation**.

E_a: see **activation energy**.

activated complex: a stage reached in a reaction where an intermediate product is formed.

activation energy (E_a): the minimum amount of kinetic energy needed by reactants before the reaction can occur.

aldehydes: flavour molecules with the carbonyl functional group on the end carbon.

amino acids: molecules with an amino group ($-NH_2$) and a carboxyl group ($-COOH$).

antioxidants: reduce the oxidation of chemicals in foods.

atom economy: compares the proportion of reactant atoms that end up in a useful product to the number that end up as waste:

$$\text{atom economy (\%)} = \frac{\text{mass of desired product}}{\text{total mass of reactants}} \times 100$$

bond enthalpy: the energy required to break one mole of bonds between the atoms in a mole of gaseous diatomic molecules, at standard temperature and pressure (25°C and 1 atmosphere).

bonding continuum: a scale that has ionic bonding at one end and pure covalent at the other, with polar covalent in between.

carbonyl group:

$$\overset{\displaystyle O}{\underset{\diagup \;\; \diagdown}{\overset{\|}{C}}}$$

chromatography: a technique which can be used to separate, identify and in some instances obtain individual substances from complex mixtures.

collision geometry: the angle at which molecules collide.

collision theory: simple collision theory states that for reactants to form products they must first come in contact with each other (collide).

concordant titres: readings which are within 0·2 cm³ of each other.

covalent network: a giant 3D structure in which all of the atoms are covalently bonded to each other.

covalent radius: half the distance between the nuclei of two atoms joined by a single covalent bond.

delocalised electrons: outer electrons which can move easily from one atom to another.

denature: breaking of hydrogen bonds in protein resulting in loss of shape of the molecules.

diols: alcohols with two hydroxyl groups.

dynamic equilibrium: the point where, in a reversible reaction, the rate of the forward reaction equals the rate of the reverse reaction.

electronegativity: the attraction an atom involved in a bond has for the electrons of the bond.

emulsifier: substance which enables normally immiscible liquids to mix.

emulsion: a mixture of two or more liquids which are normally immiscible.

energy distribution diagram: a graph of the number of molecules against kinetic energy, which shows how the energy of the reactants varies at a particular temperature.

enthalpy change (ΔH): change in energy which accompanies a chemical reaction.

enzyme: biological catalyst; most enzymes are proteins.

essential amino acids: amino acids needed by the body but which the body cannot make so gets from food.

essential oils: the concentrated extracts of the volatile non-water soluble aroma compounds found in plants.

ester link: bond formed between a carboxylic acid molecule and alcohol molecule when they react to form an ester.

fats and oils: naturally occurring esters found in animals and plants.

fatty acids: long-chain carboxylic acids found in fats and oils.

first ionisation energy: the energy required to remove one mole of electrons from one mole of atoms in the gaseous state.

fragrances: pleasant, sweet-smelling smells, caused by essential oils in plants.

free radicals: reactive particles which have unpaired electrons.

free radical chain reaction: reaction in which free radicals react in three distinct phases: (1) **initiation**: the first step where free radicals are formed when a molecule absorbs radiation. (2) **propagation**: steps where free radicals react to form further free radicals that can themselves react. (3) **termination**: step in which free radicals combine, slowing the rate and stopping the reaction.

free radical scavengers: substances that remove free radicals and stop chain reactions.

fullerene: a molecular form of carbon (C_{60}).

glycerol: propane-1,2,3-triol, an alcohol with three hydroxyl groups, found in fats and oils.

green chemistry: the design of chemical products and processes that reduce or eliminate the use and production of hazardous substances.

hydrogen bond: when hydrogen is bonded to oxygen, nitrogen or fluorine it results in a very strong permanent dipole, which in turn results in a strong permanent dipole–permanent dipole attraction between molecules called a hydrogen bond.

hydrolysis: the breaking down of a compound which involves the addition of the elements in water.

hydrophilic: water-loving.

hydrophobic: water-hating.

initiation: see **free radical chain reaction**.

intermolecular forces: attractions between molecules.

ketones: flavour molecules where the carbonyl group is not on the end carbon.

London dispersion forces: forces of attraction caused by temporary dipoles in neighbouring atoms or molecules.

mean bond enthalpy: the average bond energy, taking into account the environment of the atoms forming the bond.

miscibility: the ability of liquids to mix in all proportions, forming a solution.

molar volume (V_m): the volume occupied by one mole of a gas when measured at a given temperature and pressure.

monatomic: a substance that exists as individual non-bonded atoms (the noble gases).

oxidising agent: accepts electrons from a reactant and so oxidises it.

peptide link: bond formed between amino acids when they react – also known as the amide link.

percentage yield: compares the expected product quantity with the actual amount produced:

$$\text{percentage yield} = \frac{\text{actual yield}}{\text{theoretical yield}} \times 100$$

periodicity: repeating patterns in the periodic table.

permanent dipole–permanent dipole interactions: forces of attraction occurring between molecules with permanent dipoles.

polar covalent: the bond formed when two atoms share electrons unequally resulting in permanent dipoles.

primary alcohols: the carbon atom with the hydroxyl group is attached to **one** other carbon atom.

propagation: see **free radical chain reaction**.

proteins: natural condensation polymers made up of amino acids.

pure covalent: the bond formed when two atoms share bonding electrons equally.

R_f value: in chromatography, the distance travelled by the components of a mixture compared to the distance travelled by the solvent:

$$R_f = \frac{\text{distance travelled by compound}}{\text{distance travelled by solvent}}$$

reducing agent: supplies electrons to a reactant in order to reduce it.

reversible reaction: a reaction which can take place in both directions, i.e. the products can re-form reactants.

secondary alcohols: the carbon atom with the hydroxyl group is attached to **two** other carbon atoms.

Glossary

soap: salt of long-chain fatty acids made from fats and oils.

solvent front: the distance travelled by the solvent in chromatography.

standard enthalpy of combustion (ΔH_c): the enthalpy change when one mole of a substance burns completely, measured at standard temperature (25°C) and pressure (1 atmosphere), all substances being in their standard states.

standard solution: a solution of accurately known concentration.

sun block: mixtures containing compounds which reflect UV light and stop it reaching the skin.

termination: see **free radical chain reaction**.

terpenes: molecules that can be viewed as being based on isoprene (2-methylbuta-1, 3-diene) units joined together.

tertiary alcohols: the carbon atom with the hydroxyl group is attached to **three** other carbon atoms.

triols: alcohols with three hydroxyl groups.

ultraviolet (UV) light: high-energy radiation which causes many chemical reactions in our skin.

van der Waals forces: intermolecular forces of attraction: London dispersion forces, permanent dipole–permanent dipole interactions including hydrogen bonding.

Answers to Quick Tests

Quick Test 1

1. These forces of attraction acting between atoms of noble gases are known as London dispersion forces. They are caused by the continual movement of electrons in an atom, which causes a temporarily uneven distribution of charge at opposite sides of an atom – known as a temporary dipole. This means that one side of the atom is temporarily slightly negative (δ^-), which results in the other side being temporarily slightly positive (δ^+). This in turn induces (causes) a temporary dipole in a neighbouring atom. This results in the δ^- side of one atom attracting the δ^+ side of a neighbouring atom, so a force of attraction is formed between them.

2. (a) They both increase.

   (b) Halogens are diatomic molecules which are held together by London dispersion forces. As you go down the group the molecules have more electrons so the strength of the London dispersion forces increases. This means more energy is needed to separate the molecules so the melting and boiling points increase.

Quick Test 2

1. Sulfur consists of S_8 molecules and phosphorus P_4. The sulfur molecules have more electrons than the phosphorus molecules and so have stronger London dispersion forces. This in turn means sulfur has a higher melting point than phosphorus.

2. Fullerenes have molecules with 60 carbons or more arranged in ball shapes. The carbons are held together by covalent bonds (intramolecular forces) and the molecules are held together by London dispersion forces (intermolecular forces). Because the molecules are so big they have a large number of electrons. This results in the London dispersion forces being very strong, so a lot of energy is needed to separate the molecules, so their sublimation point is high.

3. (a) In diamond each carbon atom is covalently bonded to four other carbon atoms in a tetrahedral arrangement. All the outer electrons in the atom of each carbon are used to make single covalent bonds with neighbouring atoms, which results in a giant covalent network. In order to separate the atoms in a covalent network strong covalent bonds have to be broken, which requires a lot of energy so the sublimation point is very high.

   Sulfur is molecular and the molecules are held together by weak London dispersion forces. It does not require a lot of energy to separate the molecules so the boiling point is low compared to diamond.

   (b) In graphite each carbon atom is bonded to only three other carbon atoms. The fourth electron in each carbon atom is delocalised, so graphite can conduct electricity.

   (c) Silicon, like carbon, is in group 4 of the periodic table. Silicon forms four covalent bonds with four other silicon atoms and forms a covalent network similar to diamond.

Quick Test 3

1. (i) group (ii) radius (iii) increases (iv) nucleus (v) decreases (vi) period (vii) covalent (viii) screening (ix) stronger.

2. (a) First ionisation energy: $Mg(g) \rightarrow Mg^+(g) + e^-$
   Second ionisation energy: $Mg^+(g) \rightarrow Mg^{2+}(g) + e^-$

(b) As electrons are being removed the number of protons in the nucleus remains the same. The pull on the remaining electrons is increased, so it takes more energy to remove a second electron than the first.

(c) To remove a third electron requires much more energy as it has to be removed from an energy level closer to the nucleus, which is held more tightly than the outer electrons.

(d) $1451 + 738 = 2189$ kJ mol^{-1}

3. (i) down (ii) decreases (iii) radius (iv) electrons (v) nucleus (vi) across (vii) covalent (viii) screening (ix) stronger.

Quick Test 4

1. (i) Ionic – electronegativity difference greater than 2 (2·3)

(ii) Polar covalent – electronegativity difference less than 2 (1·0)

(iii) Polar covalent – electronegativity difference less than 2 (0·4)

2. When two atoms share bonding electrons equally it is known as pure covalent bonding. This is because they have the same attraction for the bonding electrons – both atoms have the same electronegativity value.

Atoms of elements with different electronegativity values form polar covalent bonds. This means that one atom has a greater attraction for the bonding electrons than the other. The atom with the greater attraction for the bonding electrons will have a slightly negative charge (δ^-), leaving the other atom with a slightly positive charge (δ^+). A permanent dipole is formed.

3. The type of bonding changes gradually as the difference in electronegativity between atoms changes. There is no clear distinction between covalent and ionic bonding.

Quick Test 5

1. Both have the same strength of London dispersion forces between molecules, but in addition ICl is polar covalent and so has a permanent dipole, which results in permanent dipole–permanent dipole interactions between molecules. This means more energy is needed to separate ICl molecules, so its melting point is higher.

2. (a) (i) Polar covalent

(ii) Polar

(iii) The shape of the molecule means that one side of the molecule is δ^+ and the other is δ^-. The molecule therefore has a permanent dipole.

(b) Permanent dipole–permanent dipole interactions

Quick Test 6

1. (a) (ii), (iii) and (iv)

(b) All three have hydrogen attached to the atom of a very electronegative element, which gives rise to a very polar bond. The molecules of these compounds are held together by the attraction of H$^{\delta+}$ of one molecule for the O$^{\delta-}$ or N$^{\delta-}$ or F$^{\delta-}$ of another molecule.

2. (a) (i) Around $-80°C$

(ii) Water molecules have hydrogen bonding between the molecules but the other molecules don't. More energy is needed to separate water molecules because of the hydrogen bonding.

(b) When water is cooled and reaches 4°C it begins to expand. When the water freezes and expands, the force causes the pipes to crack. This expansion of water is due to the ordering of the molecules into an open structure, with an increased number of hydrogen bonds.

3. (a) Potassium chloride exists as an ionic lattice. The water molecules interact with the ions in the lattice, break the electrostatic attraction between the ions and the ions go into solution. An electrostatic force of attraction is created between the ions and the polar water molecules – the ions are hydrated with water molecules.

   (b) Candle wax is a mixture of non-polar molecules and so water molecules can't interact with them. Heptane is a non-polar solvent. London dispersion forces can form between the molecules.

Quick Test 7

1.

	Oxidising agent	Reducing agent
(a)	$Cu^{2+}(aq)$	$Zn(s)$
(b)	$Br_2(aq)$	$2I^-(aq)$
(c)	$Ni^{2+}(aq)$	$Cr(s)$

Quick Test 8

1. (a) $Cl_2(aq) + 2e^- \rightarrow 2Cl^-(aq)$

   (b) $S_2O_3^{2-}(aq) + 5H_2O(\ell) \rightarrow 2SO_4^{2-}(aq) + 10H^+(aq) + 8e^-$

   (c) $4Cl_2(aq) + S_2O_3^{2-}(aq) + 5H_2O(\ell) \rightarrow 8Cl^-(aq) + 2SO_4^{2-}(aq) + 10H^+(aq)$

   (d) Oxidising agent: $Cl_2(aq)$; reducing agent: $S_2O_3^{2-}(aq)$

2. (a) $S_4O_6^{2-}(aq) + 2e^- \rightarrow 2S_2O_3^{2-}(aq)$ reduction

   (b) $V^{3+}(aq) + 3H_2O(\ell) \rightarrow VO_3^-(aq) + 6H^+(aq) + 2e^-$ oxidation

Quick Test 9

1. Strongest reducing agent: Li (lithium); strongest oxidising agent: F_2 (fluorine).

2. (a) (i) Yes; (ii) No; (iii) Yes; (iv) No

   (b) (i) $2I^-(aq) \rightarrow I_2(aq) + 2e^-$ oxidation

      $Br_2(aq) + 2e^- \rightarrow 2Br^-(aq)$ reduction

      (iii) $2Cl^-(aq) \rightarrow Cl_2(aq) + 2e^-$ oxidation

      $MnO_4^-(aq) + 8H^+(aq) + 5e^- \rightarrow Mn^{2+}(aq) + 4H_2O(\ell)$ reduction

   (c) (i) $2I^-(aq) + Br_2(aq) \rightarrow I_2(aq) + 2Br^-(aq)$

      (iii) $10Cl^-(aq) + 2MnO_4^-(aq) + 16H^+(aq) \rightarrow 5Cl_2(aq) + 2Mn^{2+}(aq) + 8H_2O(\ell)$

   (d) (i) Oxidising agent: $Br_2(aq)$; Reducing agent: $I^-(aq)$

      (iii) Oxidising agent: $MnO_4^-(aq)$; Reducing agent: $Cl^-(aq)$

Quick Test 10

1. 5-ethyl-2-methyloctan-3-ol

2.

Quick Test 11

1. 2,2-dimethylpentan-1-ol; primary

2.

tertiary

3. The molecules in fluoroethane are held together by weak London dispersion forces and do not need a lot of energy to separate them, so the boiling point is low. The molecules in ethanol have hydrogen bonding between them because of the –OH group on each molecule. Hydrogen bonds are stronger than London dispersion forces, so more energy is needed to separate the molecules, so the boiling point of ethanol is higher.

Quick Test 12

1. 2-ethyl-2,5-dimethylhexanoic acid

2.

3. (a) $2C_2H_5COOH + MgCO_3 \rightarrow (C_2H_5COO)_2Mg + H_2O + CO_2$

(b) Magnesium propanoate

Quick Test 13

1. (a) (i) Propyl methanoate
   (ii) Ethyl butanoate

   (b) (i)

   (ii)

2. (a)

   ethanol   ethanoic acid

   (b)

   methanoic acid   butan-2-ol

Quick Test 14

1. Glycerol has three hydroxyl groups in each molecule so can react with three fatty acid molecules.

2. Shake with bromine solution. The orange bromine rapidly loses its colour.

3. (a) In fats, the shape of the molecules allows them to pack closer together with stronger van der Waals forces between the molecules than is the case in oils. This means fats need more energy to separate the molecules, and are therefore solids at room temperature.

   (b) In a fridge the temperature is much lower than room temperature, so there is not enough energy to break the forces of attraction between the molecules, so the oil becomes solid.

Quick Test 15

1. When a fat/oil reacts with a base, salts of the fatty acids form.

2. The hydrophobic tails of the soap ions burrow into the oil and grease. The agitation causes small grease droplets (micelles) to form in the water. The negative charges on the heads prevent the globules of oil from recombining. This allows the oil or grease to be washed off the surface.

3. Detergents do not form insoluble salts (scum).

Quick Test 16

1. Emulsifiers are soap-like molecules. One or two fatty acid groups are attached to the glycerol backbone rather than the three in fats/oils. This results in the emulsifier having molecules with a hydrophobic part (the fatty acid 'tail') and a hydrophilic part – one or two hydroxyl groups or other water-soluble parts.

Quick Test 17

1. (a) (i) and (ii)

2.

Quick Test 18

1. (a)

   carvone

   (b) Ketone; the carbonyl group is not on the end carbon. The name ends in -one.

   (c) The smell of carvone (spearmint) is strong, which indicates it is volatile.

2.

Aldehyde	Ketone	
pentanal	pentan-2-one or	pentan-3-one

$C_5H_{10}O$ $C_5H_{10}O$

Quick Test 19

1. (a)

(b) $C_6H_{12}O$

(c) They have the same molecular formulae and different structures, and so are isomers. Isomers can belong to different homologous series.

2. A 4-ethyl-3-methylheptanal

   B 5,7-dimethyloctan-3-one

Quick Test 20

1. (a) (i) Acidified potassium dichromate; (ii) green; (iii) ketone; (iv) Fehling's; (v) aldehyde

   (b)

   B:

   butanone

   C:

   butanal

   (c) Carboxylic acid

2. CH_3COOH → C_2H_5OH

   O:H   1:2 (2:4)   1:6

   The O:H ratio decreases so the reaction is reduction.

Quick Test 21

1.

   butanal

   2-methyl propanal

2.

   propanal

   propanone

Quick Test 22

1. (a) Sesquiterpene

   (b)

2. (a) Oxidation

   (b)

Quick Test 23

1. (a) Free radical chain reaction

   (b) (i) Propagation; (ii) initiation; (iii) termination

   (c) UV light (radiation)

   (d) Breaking the C–Cl bond needs less energy.

Quick Test 24

1. Free radical scavengers are chemicals which react with free radicals that might otherwise cause damaging free radical chain reactions.

2. Any of the following (and also many more): vitamins C and E – foods and skin creams; polyphenols (flavonoids) – skin creams; benzophenone – plastics.

Quick Test 25

1. Waste prevention, more energy-efficient processes, reduce steps and by-products (improve the atom economy), use less hazardous and toxic chemicals, safer processes and products, design products which can be degraded in the environment, use more specific catalysts like enzymes, which reduce energy requirements.

Quick Test 26

1. (a) 30%; (b) 100%; (c) Although the percentage yield indicates low efficiency the atom economy is 100% so there are no useless by-products, which improves the overall efficiency.

2. (a) 79·8%; (b) 36·7%; (c) Although the percentage yield indicates high efficiency the atom economy is low because there are by-products, which reduces the overall efficiency.

3. £150

Quick Test 27

1. 2·1 g
2. 1·36 g

Quick Test 28

1. 0·004 mol
2. 0·225 mol l^{-1}
3. 0·02 l (20 cm^3)

Quick Test 29

1. (a) HCl by 0·003 mol
   (b) 1·22 g
2. (a) Cu by 0·03(05) mol
   (b) 13·49 g

Quick Test 30

1. (a) 3·56 l
   (b) 1·9 l
   (c) 9·86 g

Quick Test 31

1. (a) 500 cm^3
   (b) 350 cm^3
2. 1·49 l (0·0625 mol produced)

Quick Test 32

1. (a) The more particles there are, the more collisions there will be, and the greater the chance of reaction and products being formed.

   (b) Small particles offer a bigger surface area, so there are likely to be more collisions; therefore, the chance of reaction and products being formed is greater.

2. The angle at which the reactants collide can affect the rate of reaction. When diatomic molecules collide side-on, the collision is more likely to be successful than colliding end-on.

Quick Test 33

1. Sparks might be produced, which could provide the activation energy needed for the gas to react and there could be an explosion.

2. (a)

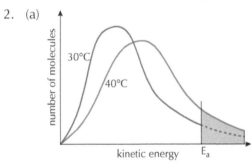

   (b) The shaded area represents the number of particles with energy equal to or greater than the activation energy for the reaction.

3. The rate of the reaction increases when the temperature is increased because more particles have a kinetic energy equal to or greater than the activation energy.

Quick Test 34

1. (a) $0.015 \ s^{-1}$

   (b) (i) Around $0.1 \ s^{-1}$

      (ii) For this reaction rate is directly proportional to concentration – doubling the concentration doubles the rate.

2. 40 s

3. $0.01 \ s^{-1}$

Quick Test 35

1. (a)

(b) Initially the reaction is very fast (the slope is steep), because there is a much larger surface area when powder is used. The larger the surface area, the more chance there is of successful collisions between reactants. As reactants are used up, the rate slows and the slope of the graph becomes less steep. Eventually the reaction stops because the acid is used up. The total volume of gas produced is the same as Experiment 1 because the same quantities are reacted – the final volume of gas is reached more quickly with powder.

Quick Test 36

1. (a) (i) -20 kJ   (ii) 15 kJ

   (b) (i) Exothermic

   (ii) The products have less PE than the reactants so energy is given out to the surroundings.

2. (a) (i) and (ii)

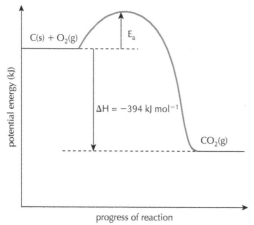

   (iii) Exothermic: indicated by $-\Delta H$ value.

(b) (i) and (ii)

(iii) Endothermic: indicated by $+\Delta H$ value.

Quick Test 37

1. (a) The activated complex is an intermediate product formed during a chemical reaction. In a PE diagram the top of the energy barrier represents the point at which the activated complex is formed.

   (b) A ---- A

   B ---- B

2. (a) Adsorption

   (b) As reactants pass over a catalyst at least one temporarily attaches to the surface of the catalyst (adsorption). The bonds in the reactant molecules weaken and new bonds form at the surface of the catalyst. Product molecules finally leave the surface of the catalyst (desorb).

   (c) A catalyst offers a reaction pathway in which each of the steps has a lower activation energy than the uncatalysed reaction, so more molecules have energy equal to or higher than the activation energy of the catalysed pathway.

Quick Test 38

1. (a) $-1676 \cdot 4$ kJ mol^{-1}

   (b) A lot of heat produced when the alcohol burns is lost to the surroundings.

2. $19 \cdot 9°C$

Quick Test 39

1. $-53 \cdot 5$ kJ mol^{-1}

2. The same reaction is happening in each case: $H^+(aq) + OH^-(aq) \rightarrow H_2O(\ell)$

Quick Test 40

1. $+51$ kJ mol^{-1}
2. -240 kJ mol^{-1}

Quick Test 41

1. -1680 kJ mol^{-1}
2. -1025 kJ mol^{-1}

Quick Test 42

1. (a) The reaction between hydrogen and iodine is reversible. As products are formed some of them re-form reactants, and an equilibrium position is reached where the rate of the forward and backward reactions is the same. At equilibrium the concentrations of reactants and products remain constant. The same equilibrium position is reached regardless of whether you start with reactants or products.

    (b) $H_2(g) + I_2(g) \rightleftharpoons 2HI(g)$

2. (a) (i) Right

    (ii) The concentration of products is greater than reactants at equilibrium.

    (b) At the point where the graphs level out.

Quick Test 43

1. (a) The equilibrium position moves left to form reactants because hydrogen ions (product) are being added, so the equilibrium moves to compensate for the imposed change.

    (b) The equilibrium position moves right. The hydroxide ions react with the hydrogen ions and so remove them. The equilibrium moves to compensate for the imposed change.

2. (a) (i) High pressure

    (ii) An increase in pressure shifts the equilibrium in the direction of fewer moles of gaseous molecules, in this case to the right, so more methanol is produced.

    (b) When a product is removed the equilibrium shifts to the right to compensate for the change, i.e. more product is formed.

Quick Test 44

1. (a) Increased yield

    (b) The forward reaction is endothermic, so is favoured by an increase in temperature (the equilibrium shifts to the right).

2. (a) The equilibrium shifts to the left.

    (b) The forward reaction is exothermic, which means the reverse reaction is endothermic, which is favoured by an increase in temperature.

3. (a) The activation energy of the reverse reaction is lowered as well as the forward reaction.

    (b) The equilibrium position is not affected, but is reached more quickly than the uncatalysed reaction.

Quick Test 45

1. (a) The forward reaction is endothermic, which is favoured by a rise in temperature. High temperature causes the equilibrium to move right.

   (b) High pressure would speed up the rate at which equilibrium is reached.

2. (a) Finely divided catalyst provides a bigger surface area on which a reaction can take place.

   (b) Removing the product causes the equilibrium position to move right, producing more ammonia.

   (c) The balanced equation shows that 1 mole of nitrogen reacts with 3 moles of hydrogen.

Quick Test 46

1. (a) A

   (b) A is more soluble in the mobile phase so will travel further up the paper.

2. (a) It is very soluble in the stationary phase or not soluble in the mobile phase.

   (b) B and C. They have components which have travelled the same distance (have the same R_f value).

3 (a) 0·38

   (b) The R_f value is constant for a particular substance if other conditions such as paper and solvent used remain the same.

Quick Test 47

1. (a) If a pen were used the solvent might separate out the mixture which makes up the ink.

   (b) To make sure that substances which didn't separate with one solvent would with the other.

2. (a) The database is used to identify unknown substances from their R_f values. If the conditions are changed after the database is set up than the R_f values will not be accurate.

   (b) Caffeine. It has the largest area under the peak.

Quick Test 48

1. (a) 0·2 g

   (b) Weigh out accurately the required mass and dissolve it in deionised water in a small beaker. Pour the solution into a volumetric flask, and rinse all of the solution out of the beaker using a water bottle. Add more deionised water until it reaches the etched line on the neck of the flask. Stopper the flask and invert it to ensure the solution is fully mixed.

2. 0·039 mol l^{-1}

3. 0·163 mol l^{-1}

Quick Test 49

1. Filtration
2. Gas syringe

Quick Test 50

1. $\dfrac{(17 \cdot 7 + 17 \cdot 9)}{2} = 17.8 \text{ cm}^3$

2. Student B

Higher
CHEMISTRY

Practice Papers

Barry McBride

Revision advice

Transfer your knowledge

As well as using the revision guide section of this book, these practice papers will also be an essential revision tool as they will help you to get used to answering exam-style questions. As you work through the questions you may find that they refer to a case study or an example that you haven't come across before. Don't worry! You should be able to transfer your knowledge of a topic or theme to a new example. The enhanced answer section which you can find online at *www.collins.co.uk/pages/Scottish-curriculum-free-resources*, will demonstrate how to read and interpret the question to identify the topic being examined and how to apply your course knowledge in order to answer the question successfully.

Command words

In the practice papers and in the exam itself, a number of command words will be used in the questions. These command words are used to tell you how you should answer a question – some words indicate that you should write more than others. If you familiarise yourself with these command words, it will help you to structure your answers more effectively. Some, but not all, of the command words you will see are explained in the table below.

Command word	Meaning/explanation
Name, state, identify, give	You only need a short answer – as a general rule you will get 1 mark for each point you give.
Suggest	You will be asked to apply your knowledge and understanding of chemistry to an unfamiliar situation.
Outline	Give a brief description or overview of what you are talking about.
Describe	Give more detail than you would in an outline, and use examples where you can.
Explain	Discuss why an action has been taken or an outcome reached – what are the reasons and/or processes behind it. If the question says 'explain fully' a more detailed explanation is required and it will be worth more marks.
Calculate or determine	Simple calculations from information given are usually worth 1 mark. More complex calculations can be worth 2 or 3 marks. It is best to show your working. In a question which says 'Find by calculation....' you must show your working.
Compare	Suggest what may happen based on available information.
Compare	Give the key features of different items or ideas and discuss their similarities and/or their differences.

In the exam

Watch your time and pace yourself carefully. Work out roughly how much time you can spend on each answer and try to stick to this. The number of marks indicates how detailed your answer should be.

Be clear before the exam what the instructions are likely to be, e.g. how many questions there are in each section. The practice papers will help you to become familiar with the exam's instructions.

Read the question thoroughly before you begin to answer it – make sure you know exactly what the question is asking you to do. If you are told to show your working then you must do so or you will not get full marks even if you have the correct answer. You will be provided with an SQA data booklet in the exam which will contain the information required to answer some of the questions.

Question types

Each paper is composed of several question types.

Knowledge-type questions include:

- Accurate recall

- Apply knowledge

- Explain

Skill-type questions include:

- Select information

- Present information

- Process information (using calculations and units, where appropriate)

- Design experiments

- Evaluate experimental procedures and suggest improvements

- Draw conclusions

- Make predictions and generalisations

In addition, there will be two open questions per paper.

Open questions

Each exam paper has two open questions and each is worth 3 marks. You can recognise an open question as it will contain the expression '**Using your knowledge of chemistry**'. In this type of question you are required to draw on your understanding of key chemical principles in order to solve a problem or challenge. The 'open-ended' nature of these questions is such that there is no one correct answer. You can be awarded 3, 2 or 1 mark depending on how well you answer the question. These questions provide you with the opportunity to be creative, and reward analytical thinking. Feel free to include diagrams to help explain your answer fully. The answer sections which you can find online at *www.collins.co.uk/pages/Scottish-curriculum-free-resources*, provide some suggestions of answers that you may include but these lists are not exhaustive and if your answer is not included within these lists it does not mean that it is incorrect.

Topic index

SQA Area	Paper A		Paper B	
Area 1 – Chemical changes and structure	**Section 1 questions**	**Section 2 questions**	**Section 1 questions**	**Section 2 questions**
Periodicity	1, 2, 20	1d, 5a	1, 4, 5, 6	2a, 2b, 2c, 2d
Structure and bonding	3, 4, 5	1a, 1b, 1c, 1e, 1f, 1g, 4a, 7, 15eiii	7, 9	7a, 7b, 9a, 13a
Oxidising and reducing agents	17, 18	9a, 10bii	20	5a, 10ai, 10aiii, 13bi
Area 2 – Nature's chemistry				
Systematic carbon chemistry	8	2a, 11b	10	6a, 6b, 12b
Alcohols and carboxylic acids	10	11b	12, 16	4a
Esters, fats and oils	9, 12			4bi, 8a, 8b, 12ci, 12cii, 12ciii
Proteins	13, 14	14b, 15c, 15ei	15	1a, 1b, 1c, 1d
Oxidation of food	11	15a, 15b, 15eiv	11, 14, 17	
Soaps, detergents, emulsion, fragrances and skin care		4c, 4d, 4ea, 14b	13	16a, 16b, 16c, 16d, 16e
Area 3 – Chemistry in society				
Getting the most from reactants	21, 22	2b, 5b, 6a, 6b, 13a, 13b, 16bi, 16biv	21, 8	4bii, 5b, 12civ, 13bii, 13ciii

Controlling the rate	7, 24	14a, 14c,	2, 3	3c, 15aii, 15b, 15c
Chemical energy	6, 19	2c, 9bi, 11a, 11c	22, 23, 24	1e, 3b, 6c, 15ai
Equilibria	15, 16	16bii, 16biii	18, 19	12a
Chemical Analysis		10bi		10b
Area 4 – Researching chemistry				
Common chemical apparatus		15d		13cii
General practical techniques	23, 25	6c, 10a, 15d	25	3a, 5c, 13ci, 13e
Reporting experimental work				10aii
Open questions	3 and 8		9b and 11	
Application of knowledge	4b, 9bii, 10c, 12a, 12b, 17a, 15eii		8c, 13d, 14	

PAPER 1 ANSWER GRID

Mark the correct answer as shown ⊙

	A	B	C	D
1	○	○	○	○
2	○	○	○	○
3	○	○	○	○
4	○	○	○	○
5	○	○	○	○
6	○	○	○	○
7	○	○	○	○
8	○	○	○	○
9	○	○	○	○
10	○	○	○	○
11	○	○	○	○
12	○	○	○	○
13	○	○	○	○
14	○	○	○	○
15	○	○	○	○
16	○	○	○	○
17	○	○	○	○
18	○	○	○	○
19	○	○	○	○
20	○	○	○	○
21	○	○	○	○
22	○	○	○	○
23	○	○	○	○
24	○	○	○	○
25	○	○	○	○

Practice Exam A

Higher Chemistry

Practice Papers for SQA Exams

Exam A

Duration – 40 minutes

Paper 1 – multiple choice

Fill in these boxes and read what is printed below.

Full name of centre

Town

Forename(s)

Surname

Total marks – 25

Attempt ALL questions.

You may use a calculator and a data booklet.

Leckie
the education publisher
for Scotland

PAPER 1 – 25 marks

Attempt ALL questions

Answers should be given on the separate answer sheet provided.

1. Carbon will form a non-polar covalent bond with an element that has an electronegativity value of

   A 1·0

   B 1·5

   C 2·2

   D 2·5.

2. What is the equation for the first ionisation of calcium?

   A $Ca(s) \longrightarrow Ca^+(s) + e^-$

   B $Ca(g) \longrightarrow Ca^+(g) + e^-$

   C $Ca(s) \longrightarrow Ca^{2+}(s) + 2e^-$

   D $Ca(g) \longrightarrow Ca^{2+}(g) + 2e^-$

3. Which of the following substances is most likely to be soluble in tetrachloromethane (CCl_4)?

   A Phosphorus chloride

   B Calcium chloride

   C Sodium chloride

   D Caesium chloride

4. What type of force is broken when ice is melted?

   A Hydrogen

   B Covalent

   C Polar covalent

   D London dispersion

5. Which of the following has a covalent molecular structure?

A Argon

B Fullerene

C Magnesium

D Graphite

6. Which line in the table correctly represents the graph shown?

	Activation energy (kJ mol^{-1})	Enthalpy change
A	180	Exothermic
B	180	Endothermic
C	100	Exothermic
D	100	Endothermic

7. In which of the following will **both** changes result in a decrease in the rate of a chemical reaction?

A An increase in activation energy and an increase in the frequency of collisions.

B An increase in activation energy and a decrease in the frequency of collisions.

C A decrease in activation energy and an increase in the frequency of collisions.

D A decrease in activation energy and a decrease in the frequency of collisions.

8. Which of the following is an isomer of methyl methanoate?

   A Methanol

   B Ethanol

   C Ethane

   D Ethanoic acid

9. Shown below is the structure of aspirin.

   Which of the following are the correct names of the two functional groups highlighted?

   A Carboxyl and ester link

   B Hydroxyl and carbonyl

   C Hydroxyl and carboxyl

   D Ester link and carbonyl

10. Which of the following structures represent a tertiary alcohol?

A

B

C

D

11. An alcohol was oxidised to produce the compound with the following structure:

Which alcohol was oxidised to produce this compound?

A Propan-1-ol

B Propanal

C Butan-1-ol

D Butan-2-ol

12. Glyceryl tristearate is a typical ester found in fats.

Hydrolysis of this compound produces 3 molecules of stearic acid and 1 molecule of

A water

B sodium stearate

C potassium stearate

D propane-1, 2, 3-triol.

13. Enzyme molecules can be classified as

A alcohols

B proteins

C esters

D fats.

14. During digestion, proteins are broken down by hydrolysis.
Which bond is broken during the hydrolysis of this protein?

A C–C

B C=O

C C–N

D N–H

15. Which of the following correctly states the effect that adding a catalyst will have on a reaction mixture at equilibrium?

A The ΔH of the reverse reaction will increase.

B The ΔH of the forward reaction will increase.

C The position of equilibrium is unchanged.

D The position of equilibrium always shifts to the right.

16. Iodine monochloride and chlorine gas react together to establish the following equilibrium in a closed system.

$$ICl(\ell) + Cl_2(g) \rightleftharpoons ICl_3(s) \qquad \Delta H = -106 \text{ kJ mol}^{-1}$$

Which line in the table shows the conditions that would result in the greatest yield of ICl_3?

	Pressure	Temperature
A	High	High
B	Low	Low
C	Low	High
D	High	Low

17. During a redox process, chlorate ions are converted into chlorine.

$$ClO_3^- \longrightarrow Cl_2$$

The reaction is carried out in acidic conditions to provide H^+ ions.

The number of moles of H^+ ions required to balance this ion–electron equation is

A 14

B 12

C 6

D 2.

18. In which of the following reactions is chlorine acting as an oxidising agent?

A $C_4H_8 + Cl_2 \longrightarrow C_4H_8Cl_2$

B $2K + Cl_2 \longrightarrow 2KCl$

C $Si + 2Cl_2 \longrightarrow SiCl_4$

D $2S + Cl_2 \longrightarrow S_2Cl_2$

19. 310 kJ of energy was released when 10 g of propan-1-ol (formula mass = 60 g) was burned.

Using this information, the enthalpy of combustion of propan-1-ol in kJ mol^{-1} is

A −52

B −155

C −1860

D −3100.

20. Which of the following elements is the strongest oxidising agent?

A Oxygen

B Fluorine

C Chlorine

D Aluminium

21. Three moles of oxygen is mixed with one mole of methane gas and ignited.

$$CH_4(g) + 2O_2(g) \longrightarrow CO_2(g) + 2H_2O(\ell)$$

Which is the correct number of moles of gas in the resulting gas mixture at room temperature?

A 1

B 2

C 3

D 4

22. Potassium chlorate can undergo thermal decomposition to produce potassium chloride and oxygen gas.

$$2KClO_3(s) \longrightarrow 2KCl(s) + 3O_2(g)$$

What volume of oxygen would be obtained by the decomposition of 0·05 moles of potassium chlorate in such a reaction?

(The molar volume of oxygen under these conditions is 24 litres mol^{-1}.)

A 1·8 litres

B 0·3 litres

C 0·15 litres

D 3·6 litres

23. The slightly water soluble gas carbon dioxide is produced when calcium carbonate and acid react together. Which of the following combinations of equipment would provide the most accurate way of measuring the volume of carbon dioxide gas produced by the reaction? (You may refer to your data booklet to help you.)

A P and Q

B S and R

C P and R

D S and Q

24. Which of the following is not a factor that affects the rate of a chemical reaction?

A Activation energy

B Concentration of reactants

C Enthalpy change of reaction

D Kinetic energy of reactant molecules

25. Which of the following procedures would be best for obtaining sodium chloride from a mixture of sodium chloride and silver chloride?

A Add water, filter and collect residue.

B Add water, filter and evaporate filtrate.

C Add hydrochloric acid, filter and collect residue.

D Add sodium hydroxide solution, filter and evaporate residue.

Higher Chemistry

Practice Papers for SQA Exams

Duration – 2 hours 20 minutes

Exam A

Paper 2

Fill in these boxes and read what is printed below.

Full name of centre

Town

Forename(s)

Surname

Total marks – 95

Attempt ALL questions.

You may use a calculator and data booklet.

the education publisher

for Scotland

Practice Papers for SQA Exams: Higher Chemistry Exam A

MARKS

DO NOT
WRITE IN
THIS
MARGIN

PAPER 2 – 95 marks

Attempt ALL questions

1. The first 20 elements of the periodic table can be categorised according to their bonding and structure.

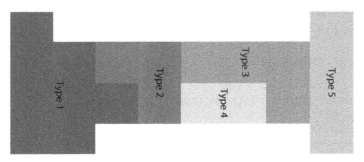

(a) Complete the following table to indicate where each type of bonding and structure can be found in the periodic table.　　　　2

Type	Bonding and structure at room temperature
	Metallic lattice solids
	Covalent network solids
	Covalent molecular gases
	Monatomic gases
	Discrete molecular solids

(b) State which type contains the element with the greatest attraction for electrons in a covalent bond.　　　　1

(c) State which type contains elements with no electronegativity values shown in the data booklet.　　　　1

(d) Explain fully why electronegativity values decrease going down a group of the periodic table.　　　　2

(continued)

MARKS

(e) Diamond and fullerene are well known forms of the element carbon. State how the structure of fullerene differs from that of diamond.

1

(f) Ionic compounds that fit the formula XY, where X is the metal ion and Y is the non-metal ion, take up one of two possible cubic arrangements.

The arrangement of the ions is determined by the radius ratio, which can be calculated using the equation shown.

$$\text{Radius ratio} = \frac{\text{Ionic radius of positive ion}}{\text{Ionic radius of negative ion}}$$

The arrangements for sodium chloride and caesium chloride are shown here.

Sodium chloride

Face-centred cubic arrangement

Radius ratio below 0·8

Caesium chloride

Body-centred cubic arrangement

Radius ratio above 0·8

(i) Calculate the radius ratio of magnesium oxide.

You may wish to use your data booklet to help.

1

(ii) State which cubic arrangement magnesium oxide would take.

1

(g) Explain fully why caesium chloride has more ionic character than sodium chloride.

2

2. The rocket propellant dinitrogen tetroxide was developed in the 1950s.

In rockets it reacts with methylhydrazine.

$$5N_2O_4 + 4CH_3NHNH_2 \longrightarrow XCO_2 + YN_2 + ZH_2O$$

(methylhydrazine)

(a) Draw the full structural formula of methylhydrazine.

1

(b) Balance the above equation by giving the values of X, Y and Z.

1

(c) The equations for the combustion of methylhydrazine, carbon and hydrogen are:

$CH_3NHNH_2(\ell) + 2\frac{1}{2}O_2(g) \longrightarrow CO_2(g) + N_2(g) + 3H_2O(\ell)$ $\Delta H = -1304$ kJ mol^{-1}

$C(s) + O_2(g) \longrightarrow CO_2(g)$ $\Delta H = -394$ kJ mol^{-1}

$H_2(g) + \frac{1}{2}O_2(g) \longrightarrow H_2O(\ell)$ $\Delta H = -286$ kJ mol^{-1}

Use this information to calculate the enthalpy change, in kJ mol^{-1}, if methylhydrazine could be made directly from its elements.

$C(s) + N_2(g) + 3H_2(g) \longrightarrow CH_3NHNH_2(\ell)$ $\Delta H = ?$

Show your working clearly.

3

MARKS

DO NOT
WRITE IN
THIS
MARGIN

Practice Papers for SQA Exams: Higher Chemistry Exam A

3. Vinaigrette salad dressing can be made using the following ingredients:

Ingredients
Olive oil
Salt
Vinegar (ethanoic acid)
Dijon mustard (emulsifier)
Water

Using your knowledge of chemistry, comment on how the ingredients present in the vinaigrette dressing will interact with each other.

3

4. X-ray diffraction is a technique used to determine the structures of molecules. The scattering intensity of an X-ray beam hitting a sample allows us to determine the shape of a molecule. An example is shown:

Full structural formula of phenol   Electron density map over molecule   X-ray electron density map

Phenol, C_6H_5OH

(a) The hydrogen atoms do not show up clearly on an electron density map. Suggest a reason for this.

1

(b) Shown below is an electron density map over a different molecule.

Draw the full structural formula of this molecule.

1

Compounds containing a ring structure, such as limonene shown below, are often associated with strong smelling compounds.

(c) Limonene is a colourless or pale yellow liquid with a sweet lemon-like odour. It occurs naturally in many essential oils, which can be used in cosmetic products.

To which group of compounds does limonene belong?

1

MARKS

DO NOT WRITE IN THIS MARGIN

(continued)

(d) Limonene can be produced by joining together isoprene units.

Give the systematic name of isoprene. **1**

(e) (i) Many cosmetic products also contain free radical scavengers.

State what is meant by the term 'free radical scavengers'. **1**

(ii) Free radical chain reactions involve three steps.

State the names of the three steps. **1**

5. Sulfur is removed from impure blast furnace iron by the addition of magnesium powder. Magnesium sulfide is formed, which then floats on top of the molten iron and is removed.

$$Mg + S \longrightarrow MgS$$

(a) (i) Explain fully the difference in size between an atom of sulfur and an atom of magnesium. **2**

(ii) Write the equation for the second ionisation enthalpy of magnesium. **1**

(continued)

MARKS

(b) Calculate the theoretical mass, in kilograms, of magnesium sulfide that would be produced by adding 100 kg of magnesium to excess sulfur.

Show your working clearly.   2

6. An investigation into the use of metals to produce hydrogen was carried out.

   2·0 g of lead was added to 10 cm^3 of 1 mol l^{-1} hydrochloric acid to generate hydrogen gas.

   The balanced equation for the reaction is:

$$Pb(s) + 2HCl(aq) \longrightarrow PbCl_2(aq) + H_2(g)$$

   (a) (i) Show by calculation which reactant is in excess.

   Show your working clearly.   2

   (ii) Calculate the mass of hydrogen gas which will have been given off during the experiment.

   Show your working clearly.   1

MARKS

DO NOT
WRITE IN
THIS
MARGIN

Practice Papers for SQA Exams: Higher Chemistry Exam A

(continued)

(b) The hydrogen produced in the reaction can be contaminated with hydrogen chloride vapour, which is very soluble in water.

Complete the following diagram to show how the hydrogen chloride could be removed before the hydrogen is collected.

1

7. The table shown compares the properties of ethanol and propane.

Hydrocarbon	Boiling point	State at room temperature	Solubility in water	Formula mass
Ethanol	78·4°C	liquid	soluble	46
Propane	−42°C	gas	insoluble	44

Explain fully why, although propane and ethanol have very similar formula masses, they have very different properties.

You should give mention to both the bonding and intermolecular forces involved and how they arise.

4

8. Manufacturers of scented soap products suggest that soap should be stored in cool, dry conditions when not in use to prolong the life of the soap and to maintain its scent.

   Using your knowledge of chemistry, comment on why the soap should be stored in cool, dry conditions.

   3

9. Car companies are developing fuel cells as a replacement for conventional petrol and diesel engines to power their vehicles.

   Initially car companies were looking at methanol fuel cells, but they found some disadvantages with those when compared to hydrogen fuel cells.

   (a) The ion–electron equations for both the oxidation and the reduction reactions that take place in a methanol fuel cell are:

   $$CH_3OH(\ell) + H_2O(\ell) \longrightarrow CO_2(g) + 6H^+(aq) + 6e^-$$
   $$3O_2(g) + 12H^+(aq) + 12e^- \longrightarrow 6H_2O(\ell)$$

   Combine the two ion–electron equations to give the equation for the overall redox reaction.

   1

MARKS

(continued)

(b) (i) The equation for the reaction in a hydrogen fuel cell is:

$$2H_2(g) + O_2(g) \longrightarrow 2H_2O(\ell)$$

Using bond enthalpy values, calculate the enthalpy change, in kJ mol^{-1} for the reaction.

Show your working clearly.

2

(ii) Suggest a disadvantage of using a methanol fuel cell when compared to a hydrogen fuel cell.

1

10. Acidified potassium permanganate can be used to determine the concentration of iron(II) sulfate solution by titration.

(a) (i) A standard solution of potassium permanganate is required to perform the titration.

State what is meant by the term 'standard solution'.

1

(ii) Describe how a standard solution is prepared from a weighed sample of potassium permanganate.

3

MARKS

DO NOT
WRITE IN
THIS
MARGIN

Practice Papers for SQA Exams: Higher Chemistry Exam A

(continued)

(b) (i) An average of 10·1 cm³ of 1 mol l⁻¹ potassium permangante solution was required to completely react with 20 cm³ of iron(II) sulfate solution.

The equation for this reaction is:

$$5Fe^{2+}(aq) + MnO_4^-(aq) + 8H^+(aq) \longrightarrow 5Fe^{3+}(aq) + Mn^{2+}(aq) + 4H_2O(\ell)$$

Calculate the concentration, in mol l⁻¹, of the iron(II) sulfate solution.

Show your working clearly.   3

(ii) State why no indicator is required for this titration.   1

(c) The recommended daily allowance (RDA) for iron is 27 mg for pregnant women.

A breakfast cereal provides 3·6 mg of iron per 30 g of cereal.

Calculate the percentage of the RDA that is provided by 100 g of this cereal.   2

MARKS

DO NOT
WRITE IN
THIS
MARGIN

Practice Papers for SQA Exams: Higher Chemistry Exam A

11. The enthalpy of combustion of ethanol can be obtained using the apparatus shown.

(a) (i) In the experiment it was found that burning 0·64 g of ethanol increased the temperature of the water by 10·0°C.

Calculate the enthalpy of combustion, in kJ mol⁻¹, of ethanol.

Show your working clearly. 3

(ii) State the measurements required to calculate the mass of ethanol burned in this experiment. 1

(iii) The theoretical value for the enthalpy of combustion of ethanol is much higher than the experimental value.

Suggest why the experimental value is different to the theoretical value. 1

MARKS

DO NOT
WRITE IN
THIS
MARGIN

Practice Papers for SQA Exams: Higher Chemistry Exam A

(continued)

(b) The energy density value of a fuel is the energy released when one kilogram of the fuel is completely burned.

The enthalpy of combustion of ethanol stated in the data book is −1367 kJ mol⁻¹.

Calculate the energy density value, in kJ kg⁻¹, of ethanol.

Show your working clearly. 1

(c) The enthalpy change for this reaction can also be calculated using bond enthalpies and mean bond enthalpies.

Explain the difference between bond enthalpy and mean bond enthalpy. 1

12. The Born–Haber cycle is an approach to analysing the energies involved in chemical reactions. Born–Haber cycles are used as a means of calculating lattice enthalpies, which cannot otherwise be measured directly. An example is shown below.

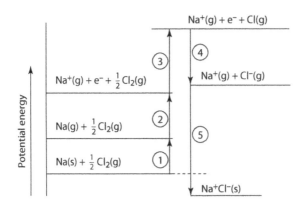

(continued)

    (a) State which of the five reaction stages involves the greatest release of energy.   **1**

    (b) Write an equation for the overall reaction that is represented by this Born–Haber cycle.   **1**

13. Calcium carbonate reacts with sulfuric acid to produce calcium sulfate for use in making plaster.

$$H_2SO_4(aq) + CaCO_3(s) \longrightarrow CaSO_4(aq) + CO_2(g) + H_2O(\ell)$$

    (a) 490 tonnes of calcium carbonate was used to produce 550 tonnes of calcium sulfate.

    Calculate the percentage yield.

    Show your working clearly.   **3**

    (b) Calculate the atom economy for this reaction.

    Show your working clearly.   **2**

14. The enzyme catalase increases the rate of the decomposition of hydrogen peroxide.

The equation for this reaction is:

$$2H_2O_2(aq) \longrightarrow 2H_2O(\ell) + O_2(g)$$

(a) It was established that the relative rate of this reaction at 30 °C was 0·025 s^{-1}.
Calculate the time taken for the reaction at 30 °C.

1

(b) Enzymes are biological catalysts.

State the name of the functional group found in all enzymes.

1

(c) The potential energy diagram below shows the change in potential energy during the reaction carried out without a catalyst.

(i) Draw an X on the potential energy diagram above to show where the activated complex is formed.

1

(ii) Add a dotted line to the diagram to show the change in potential energy when the enzyme is added.

1

(d) Draw a labelled diagram to show how the course of this reaction could be followed.

2

15. In the production of cheese the oxidation of alcohols is promoted, however the oxidation of alcohols in the production of wine is prevented to stop the wine going off.

Ketones, such as heptan-2-one, are responsible for the smell associated with blue cheese. These ketones are only found in the cheese after a ripening process has been undertaken.

(a) Name the functional group present in heptan-2-one.

1

(b) Name the alcohol that can be oxidised to produce heptan-2-one.

1

(c) Proteins in milk are broken down first into peptides, then amino acids, and finally converted into a range of other molecules contributing to the taste and smell of the cheese.

MARKS

DO NOT
WRITE IN
THIS
MARGIN

Practice Papers for SQA Exams: Higher Chemistry Exam A

(continued)

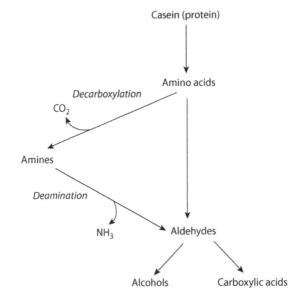

(i) Name the reaction that turns proteins into amino acids. **1**

(ii) Decarboxylation turns amino acids into amines, which are compounds that only contain an amino group.

Draw the structure of the amine produced on decarboxylation of the amino acid glycine. **1**

(d) The mixtures of amino acids produced were separated using paper chromatography.

(continued)

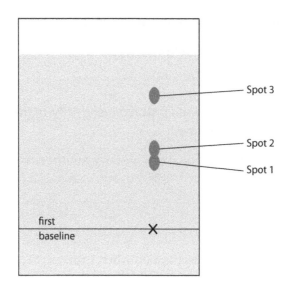

The retention factor, Rf, for a substance can be calculated using the equation

$$Rf = \frac{\text{distance moved by the substance}}{\text{maximum distance moved by the solvent}}$$

(i) Identify the spot with the highest Rf value.

1

(ii) Explain why different amino acids travel different distances up the
chromatography paper.

1

In the wine-making process the sugars found in grapes are converted into alcohol.
Brewers add yeast to the crushed grapes which increases the rate of production of the
alcohol.

(e) Yeast contains enzymes which convert the sugars into alcohol and carbon
dioxide in a process known as fermentation.

(i) State what is meant by the term 'enzyme'.

1

(ii) The percentage by mass of alcohol in the wine can be calculated using the
formula

1

$$\% \text{ by mass of alcohol} = \frac{\text{mass of alcohol}}{\text{mass of wine}} \times 100$$

A 20 cm³ sample of wine was found to contain 2·12 g of alcohol and 1 cm³ of the wine
weighed 0·99 g.

Calculate the percentage by mass of alcohol in the wine.

(continued)

    (iii) The process of fermentation produces ethanol.

        Explain **fully** why ethanol is soluble in water.   **2**

    (iv) Ethanol in wine can be oxidised if stored incorrectly. In the first stage of this two-stage process ethanal is formed.

        Further oxidation of the ethanal can produce another chemical which affects the taste of the wine.

        Name this product.   **1**

16. Fumaric acid is produced naturally by the skin when exposed to sunlight.

$$HOOC\diagdown_{H} C = C \diagup^{H}_{\diagdown COOH}$$

(a) In the lab fumaric acid can be reacted with bromine.

    (i) State the name of the reaction that takes place between fumaric acid and bromine.   **1**

    (ii) State the colour change that would be observed in this reaction.   **1**

(b) Fumaric acid can also be used to prepare esters using the method shown.

Fumaric acid, alcohol and catalyst

(i) State the number of moles of ethanol that can react with one mole of fumaric acid.

1

(ii) Name the type of reaction that takes place between fumaric acid and an alcohol.

1

(iii) Name the catalyst used in this reaction.

1

(iv) The reaction mixture must be heated for the reaction to take place. Suggest how the reaction mixture should be heated.

1

(c) The structure of the alcohol used to produce the ester is shown.

(i) Give the systematic name of the alcohol used.

1

(ii) The alcohol also reacts with acidified potassium dichromate.

State the colour change that would be observed when the alcohol reacts with acidified potassium dichromate.

1

(iii) Draw the full structural formula of the product of this reaction.

1

PAPER 1 ANSWER GRID

Mark the correct answer as shown ◉

	A	B	C	D
1	○	○	○	○
2	○	○	○	○
3	○	○	○	○
4	○	○	○	○
5	○	○	○	○
6	○	○	○	○
7	○	○	○	○
8	○	○	○	○
9	○	○	○	○
10	○	○	○	○
11	○	○	○	○
12	○	○	○	○
13	○	○	○	○
14	○	○	○	○
15	○	○	○	○
16	○	○	○	○
17	○	○	○	○
18	○	○	○	○
19	○	○	○	○
20	○	○	○	○
21	○	○	○	○
22	○	○	○	○
23	○	○	○	○
24	○	○	○	○
25	○	○	○	○

Practice Exam B

Higher Chemistry

Practice Papers for SQA Exams

Duration – 40 minutes

Exam B

Paper 1

Fill in these boxes and read what is printed below.

Full name of centre

Town

Forename(s)

Surname

Total marks – 25

Attempt ALL questions.

You may use a calculator and data booklet.

PAPER 1 – 25 marks

Attempt ALL questions

Answers should be given on the separate answer sheet provided.

1. Which of the following chlorides has the **most** ionic character?

   A NaCl

   B CsCl

   C $CaCl_2$

   D $AlCl_3$

2. The average kinetic energy of particles in a substance is measured with a

   A pipette

   B burette

   C thermometer

   D standard flask.

3. A small increase in the temperature of a reaction mixture results in a large increase in the reaction rate. The main reason for this is

   A the activation energy is lowered

   B the enthalpy change is increased

   C the enthalpy change is decreased

   D the kinetic energy of the particles is increased.

4. The element francium occurs in Group 1 of the periodic table. Of all the elements in Group 1, francium will have the

   A highest first ionisation energy

   B lowest electronegativity

   C smallest covalent radius

   D lowest relative atomic mass.

5. Which of the following reactions represents the first ionisation energy of chlorine?

A $Cl_2(\ell) + e^- \longrightarrow Cl^-(g)$

B $Cl_2(g) + 2e^- \longrightarrow 2Cl^-(g)$

C $Cl(g) \longrightarrow Cl^+(g) + e^-$

D $Cl(g) \longrightarrow Cl^{2+}(g) + 2e^-$

6. The difference between the covalent radius of sodium and chlorine is mainly due to the difference in the

A number of energy levels

B number of neutrons

C number of protons

D mass of each atom.

7. An unknown element is found to have a melting point of over 2000°C, but an oxide of this element is a gas at room temperature.

Which of the following types of bonding is most likely to be present in the element?

A Metallic

B Pure covalent

C Ionic

D Polar covalent

8. The number of moles of ions in 1 mole of iron(II) phosphate is

A 2

B 3

C 4

D 5.

9. Which of the following compounds has polar molecules?

A

B

C $O\!=\!C\!=\!O$

D

CI
|
CI''''''C
       \CI
CI

10. Which of the following compounds is not an isomer of pentanoic acid?

A Methyl butanoate

B Ethyl propanoate

C Propyl ethanoate

D Methyl pentanoate

11. Which of the following compounds is a ketone?

A

B

C

D

12. Glycerol is a chemical compound also commonly called glycerin or glycerine. Which of the following is the correct systematic name for glycerol?

A Propan-2-ol

B Propane-1,2,3-triol

C Propanoic acid

D Propyl propanoate

13. Emulsifiers are commonly added to food to

A reduce calorific value

B reduce saturated fat value

C prevent oxidation

D prevent oil and water molecules from separating.

14. Which of the following can be classified as an ester?

A Fat

B Soap

C Glycerol

D Fatty acid

15. Amino acids are converted into proteins by

A addition

B hydrolysis

C esterification

D condensation.

16. Paracetamol is a widely used pain reliever. The structure of paracetamol is shown.

Which two functional groups are highlighted in the structure of paracetamol?

A Amide link and hydroxyl

B Hydroxyl and carbonyl

C Amino and carbonyl

D Amino and carboxyl

17. Which of the following could be prepared by reacting a secondary alcohol with acidified potassium dichromate solution?

A

$$\underset{O}{\overset{H}{\underset{\diagdown}{C}}} - H$$

B

$$\underset{O}{\overset{CH_3}{\underset{\diagdown}{C}}} - CH_3$$

C

$$\underset{O}{\overset{HO}{\underset{\diagdown}{C}}} - CH_3$$

D

$$\underset{O}{\overset{CH_3 - O}{\underset{\diagdown}{C}}} - CH_3$$

18. In a reversible reaction, equilibrium is established when

A the concentration of the reactants and products is equal

B the concentration of the reactants and products is constant

C the concentration of only the products remains unchanged

D the concentration of only the reactants remains unchanged.

19. In which of the following reactions would a change in pressure **not** affect the yield of product?

A $ICl(\ell) + Cl_2(g) \rightleftharpoons ICl_3(s)$

B $2NO_2(g) \rightleftharpoons N_2O_4(g)$

C $H_2(g) + I_2(g) \rightleftharpoons 2HI(g)$

D $N_2(g) + 3H_2(g) \rightleftharpoons 2NH_3(g)$

20. Stannic chloride ($SnCl_4$) was used in World War I as a chemical weapon due to its corrosive and toxic properties. It can be produced by the reaction shown.

$$HgCl_2 + SnCl_2 \longrightarrow Hg + SnCl_4$$

Which of the following ions is oxidised in the above reaction?

A Sn^{2+}

B Sn^{4+}

C Hg^{2+}

D Cl^-

21. The equation for the complete combustion of methane is shown below.

$$CH_4(g) + 2O_2(g) \longrightarrow CO_2(g) + 2H_2O(\ell)$$

If 20 cm³ of methane is ignited and burned with 100 cm³ of oxygen, what is the volume of the resulting gas mixture?

A 20 cm³

B 50 cm³

C 80 cm³

D 120 cm³

22. State the enthalpy of formation of carbon monoxide (reaction X) using the reaction pathway shown.

A −110 kJ mol⁻¹

B +110 kJ mol⁻¹

C −678 kJ mol⁻¹

D +678 kJ mol⁻¹

23. Molar bond enthalpy is the energy required to

A break one mole of bonds in a diatomic molecule

B convert one mole of reactants into one mole of products

C remove an electron from one mole of atoms in the gaseous state

D break one mole of bonds for a bond that occurs in a number of compounds.

24. The enthalpy of combustion is always the energy released when

A 1 mole of a substance is completely burned in excess oxygen

B an excess of substance is burned in 1 mole of oxygen

C 1 g of a substance is completely burned in excess oxygen

D an excess of substance is burned in 1 g of oxygen.

25. In chromatography, the identity of a component can be indicated either by the distance it has travelled or by the time it has taken to travel through the apparatus. The time taken is called the

A reaction time

B relation time

C resultant time

D retention time.

Higher Chemistry

Practice Papers for SQA Exams

Duration – 2 hours 20 minutes

Exam B

Paper 2

Fill in these boxes and read what is printed below.

Full name of centre

Town

Forename(s)

Surname

Total marks – 95

Attempt ALL questions.

You may use a calculator and a data booklet.

MARKS

PAPER 2 – 95 marks

Attempt ALL questions

1. Phenylalanine is an essential amino acid which is found naturally in the breast milk of mammals.

(a) State what is meant by the term 'essential amino acid'. **1**

alanine

(b) Alanine, another amino acid, can combine with phenylalanine to form a dipeptide. Draw a possible full structural formula of the molecule formed when one molecule of alanine joins with one molecule of phenylalanine. **1**

MARKS

DO NOT
WRITE IN
THIS
MARGIN

Practice Papers for SQA Exams: Higher Chemistry Exam B

(continued)

(c) Name the link which holds amino acids together in a protein molecule.

1

(d) Proteins can be denatured by heat.

State what is meant by the term 'denatured'.

1

(e) Proteins called enzymes can be used to catalyse the breakdown of hydrogen peroxide into water and oxygen as shown by the following equation:

$$2H \overset{O-O}{<} H \rightarrow 2H \overset{O}{<} H + O=O$$

The bond enthalpy of an oxygen-to-oxygen single bond is 142 kJ mol⁻¹. Use this information and the bond enthalpy values given in the data booklet to calculate the enthalpy change, in kJ mol⁻¹ for the reaction.

Show your working clearly.

3

MARKS

DO NOT
WRITE IN
THIS
MARGIN

Practice Papers for SQA Exams: Higher Chemistry Exam B

2. Patterns in electronegativity, covalent radius and ionisation enthalpy can all be found in the periodic table.

(a) State what is meant by the term 'electronegativity'.

1

(b) Explain fully why electronegativity decreases going down a group in the periodic table.

2

(c) Explain fully the trend in covalent radius going across the periodic table from potassium to krypton.

2

(d) **Explain fully** why the first ionisation enthalpy of sodium is less than the first ionisation enthalpy of lithium.

2

MARKS

3. The effect of changing the temperature on the rate of a reaction can be studied using the following reaction.

$$5(COOH)_2(aq) + 6H^+(aq) + 2MnO_4^-(aq) \longrightarrow 2Mn^{2+}(aq) + 10CO_2(g) + 8H_2O(\ell)$$

(a) Draw a diagram to show how the rate of this reaction could be monitored in the lab.

2

(b) **Explain fully** why increasing the temperature results in an increase in the rate of a chemical reaction.

2

(c) The graph shown illustrates the kinetic energy for molecules at a certain temperature.

Draw a new line on the graph that you would expect to see if the temperature was increased.

1

4. Citric acid is a preservative which occurs naturally in citrus fruits and can also be added to food and drinks to give an acidic or sour taste.

(a) **Explain fully**, with reference to the structure of citric acid, why it is very soluble in water.

2

(b) Citrus fruits also contain esters, which are partly responsible for the flavour of the fruit.

The ester shown is found in pineapples.

(i) Give the name of the ester.

1

(ii) A student produced this ester in the lab and obtained a yield of 65%.

Calculate the mass of the ester (formula mass 130 g) the student produced if they reacted 22·2 g of alcohol (formula mass 32 g).

Show your working clearly.

3

5. Carbon monoxide is a tasteless, colourless but highly toxic gas and yet despite this it was once used as a domestic fuel.

   Carbon monoxide can be produced by reacting zinc with calcium carbonate.

   $$Zn + CaCO_3 \longrightarrow ZnO + CaO + CO$$

   (a) Write the ion–electron equation for the oxidation step in the reaction.

   State symbols are not required.　　**1**

   (b) Calculate the atom economy for the formation of carbon monoxide in this reaction.

   Show your working clearly.　　**2**

   (c) Carbon monoxide can also be produced in the lab as a product of the reaction of carbon dioxide with hot carbon.

   The carbon dioxide is made by the reaction of dilute hydrochloric acid with solid calcium carbonate. Unreacted carbon dioxide is removed before the carbon monoxide is collected by displacement of water.

   Stage 1 　　　　　　　　　　　　　　Stage 2

   The required carbon dioxide is produced in stage 1 and the excess carbon dioxide is removed using limewater in stage 2.

   Complete the diagrams for stage 1 and 2.　　**2**

6. Alkynes are a family of hydrocarbons that contain a carbon-to-carbon triple bond in their structures.

The first member of the alkynes is ethyne, which has the formula C_2H_2.

(a) Alkynes can undergo addition reactions, which involve the addition of a diatomic molecule across a triple or double bond.

One example is shown:

$$H-C\equiv C-H \xrightarrow{\quad HCl \quad} \text{Compound X} \xrightarrow{\quad HCl \quad} \text{Compound Y}$$

Draw a possible full structural formula for compounds X and Y.

2

(b) Ethanol can also be produced from ethyne by an addition reaction with water. The ethanol produced can undergo oxidation.

Name compounds A and B.

2

Practice Papers for SQA Exams: Higher Chemistry Exam B

MARKS

DO NOT
WRITE IN
THIS
MARGIN

(continued)

(c) The equation for the enthalpy of formation of ethyne is:

$$2C(s) + H_2(g) \longrightarrow C_2H_2(g)$$

Use the enthalpies of combustion of ethyne, carbon and hydrogen given below to calculate the enthalpy of formation of ethyne, in kJ mol^{-1}.

$C_2H_2(g) + 2\frac{1}{2}O_2(g) \longrightarrow 2CO_2(g) + H_2O(\ell)$ $\Delta H = -1301$ kJ mol^{-1}

$C(s) + O_2(g) \longrightarrow CO_2(g)$ $\Delta H = -394$ kJ mol^{-1}

$H_2(g) + \frac{1}{2}O_2(g) \longrightarrow H_2O(\ell)$ $\Delta H = -286$ kJ mol^{-1}

Show your working clearly.   2

7. The properties of four different substances are shown in the table.

Substance	Melting point (°C)	Boiling point (°C)	Solubility in water	Conduction of electricity
A	−77	−33	Insoluble	Non-conductor
B	1414	3265	Insoluble	Conductor
C	405	482	Soluble	Only when molten
D	660	2519	Insoluble	Non-conductor

(a) Complete the table below by using the letters to show the type of bonding and structure present in each substance.   2

Substance	Bonding and structure
	Metallic
	Ionic
	Covalent molecular
	Covalent network

(b) Ethane has a boiling point of −89°C, however methanol has a boiling point of 65°C.

Explain fully why methanol has a high boiling point relative to ethane.

3

8. Hydrogenation results in the conversion of liquid vegetable oils to solid or semi-solid fats, such as those present in margarine.

(a) Explain fully why fats have a higher melting point than oils.

2

(b) Name the class of organic compound found in fats and oils.

1

(continued)

(c) A margarine contains 0·1 g of sodium per 10 g of margarine. The sodium is present in the margarine as sodium chloride.

Calculate the mass of sodium chloride, in g, present in a 500 g tub of margarine.

Show your working clearly.

2

9. 'When I was 9 years old, my parents gave me a chemistry set. Within a week, I had decided to become a chemist and never wavered from that choice', recalled Robert F. Curl, Jr in his Nobel Prize autobiography. Curl Jr was awarded the Nobel Prize in Chemistry in 1996 for the discovery of fullerenes, and was one of the many Nobel Prize winners who credit the kits for inspiring their career.

(a) Complete the table to show the various bonding and structures of the two forms of carbon.

1

Form of carbon	Bonding	Structure at room temperature
Fullerenes		
Diamond		

MARKS

DO NOT
WRITE IN
THIS
MARGIN

Practice Papers for SQA Exams: Higher Chemistry Exam B

(continued)

(b) Sales of chemistry sets have increased in recent years. The chemistry set shown is designed for use on typical foods found in the home.

Chemistry of Food Experiment Kit

6 large test tubes

Test tube rack

Biuret reagent (protein indicator)

Benedict's solution (glucose indicator)

Lugol's iodine (starch indicator)

Indophenol (vitamin C indicator)

Ascorbic acid (vitamin C)

Copper(II) oxide

Pipette (dropper)

250 ml glass beaker

Experiment guide with charts to record test results

Using your knowledge of chemistry, suggest some experiments and expected results that may be included in the experiment guide.

3

10. Hydrogen peroxide is used medically as an antiseptic for cleaning wounds. The concentration of a hydrogen peroxide solution can be calculated by titration with acidified potassium permanganate.

The reaction is represented by the equation:

$$2MnO_4^-(aq) + 6H^+(aq) + 5H_2O_2(aq) \longrightarrow 2Mn^{2+}(aq) + 8H_2O(\ell) + 5O_2(g)$$

25 cm^3 of hydrogen peroxide was titrated with a 0·1 mol l^{-1} acidified potassium permanganate solution and the results are shown in the table.

Titration	Volume of potassium permanganate/ (cm$_3$)
1	16·2
2	15·7
3	15·9

(a) (i) Suggest why the potassium permanganate solution is acidified.   1

(ii) State why no indicator is required in this titration.   1

(iii) Name the type of reaction taking place.   1

(b) Use the results shown in the table to calculate the concentration, in mol l^{-1}, of the hydrogen peroxide solution.

Show your working clearly.   3

MARKS

11. Household drains are most commonly blocked by fat, soap and protein deposits such as hair.

One of the most common substances used to unblock drains is a solution of caustic soda (sodium hydroxide), which can break down these substances.

Using your knowledge of chemistry, comment on the reactions that may be taking place when the caustic soda reacts with substances causing the blockage.

3

12. Synthesis gas is a mixture of hydrogen and carbon monoxide and can be prepared as shown below.

Nickel is known to catalyse the reaction.

$$CH_4(g) + H_2O(g) \rightleftharpoons 3H_2(g) + CO(g)$$

(a) (i) An increase in temperature increases the yield of synthesis gas.

State the type of enthalpy change for the forward reaction.

1

MARKS

DO NOT WRITE IN THIS MARGIN

(continued)

(ii) Explain fully how a change in pressure will affect the composition of the equilibrium mixture.

2

(iii) State how the composition of the equilibrium mixture would be affected by the use of the catalyst.

1

(b) A reaction sequence involving an addition reaction between synthesis gas and propene is shown:

$$2H_2(g) + 2CO(g) + 2C_3H_6(g) \longrightarrow CH_3CH_2CH_2CHO(\ell) + \text{compound B}$$
compound A

compound A → butan-1-ol

compound B → alcohol C

Compound A and compound B are isomers of different types of organic compound.

(i) Name the type of organic compounds to which compound B belongs.

1

(ii) Draw the full structural formula of compound B and name it.

2

MARKS

DO NOT
WRITE IN
THIS
MARGIN

Practice Papers for SQA Exams: Higher Chemistry Exam B

(continued)

(iii) Give the name of the reagent required if pentan-1-ol was required as a product.

1

(c) (i) Name the type of chemical reaction which would occur if hexan-1-ol reacted with ethanoic acid.

1

(ii) Draw the full structural formula for the product of this reaction.

1

(iii) Give a possible use for this product.

1

(iv) Suggest why obtaining a percentage yield of 100% of this product would be difficult.

1

MARKS

13. Tin metal, when heated, reacts with chlorine gas to form tin(IV) chloride, $SnCl_4$, a colourless liquid (b.p. 114°C).

(a) State the type of bonding in tin(IV) chloride.

1

(b) The main source of tin is the ore cassiterite or tinstone, SnO_2. After preliminary treatment the concentrated ore is heated in a furnace with coke (carbon) at about 1200°C.

$$SnO_2(s) + C(s) \longrightarrow Sn(s) + CO_2(g)$$

(i) Name the reducing agent in this reaction.

1

(ii) Calculate the volume of carbon dioxide produced in this reaction if 500 g of cassiterite is completely converted to tin.

Take the molar volume to be 24 litres mol^{-1}.

Show your working clearly.

3

(c) A student investigated the purity of a sample of tin(IV) chloride.

The sample was dissolved in deionised water and to this an excess of silver nitrate was added, which produced a precipitate of silver chloride.

The precipitate was dried and then weighed.

(i) Explain why the student used deionised water to dissolve the tiv(IV) chloride sample. **1**

(ii) Give the name of the most appropriate piece of apparatus that could be used to measure

(A) accurately 20·0 cm³ of zinc(IV) chloride.

Equipment _____

(B) approximately 35 cm³ of silver chloride solution.

Equipment _____ **2**

(iii) 3·33 g of silver chloride was precipitated from the zinc(IV) chloride solution.

$$ZnCl_4(aq) + 4AgNO_3(aq) \longrightarrow Zn(NO_3)_4(aq) + 4AgCl(s)$$

Calculate the mass, in grams, of zinc(IV) chloride in the sample. **3**

(d) The average mass of zinc(IV) chloride in 12 g of the original sample was 9·6 g.

Calculate the percentage of zinc(IV) chloride present in the original sample. **1**

(e) Name the two separation techniques that must be used to separate the precipitate of silver chloride from the reaction mixture. **1**

14. The crystal structure of an ionic compound is determined by the 'radius ratio' of the ions involved.

$$\text{Radius ratio} = \frac{\text{Ionic radius of positive ion}}{\text{Ionic radius of negative ion}}$$

Explain fully, showing your working, why magnesium oxide is likely to have the same crystal structure as sodium chloride.

(You may use your data booklet to help you.)　　　　　　　　　　　2

15. The diagram below shows the energy changes for the reaction

A + B　　　⟶　　　C + D

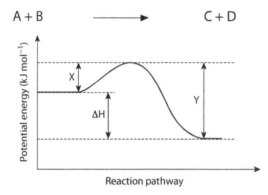

(a) (i) Using the symbols X and Y from the diagram, write a simple equation to show how the enthalpy change for the forward reaction could be calculated.　　1

　　(ii) State how the values of X and Y could be decreased with no change in ΔH.　　1

(b) Suggest why some collisions of particles A and B result in no reaction.　　1

(c) State the name given to the unstable arrangement of atoms formed during a reaction. **1**

16. The chlorine atoms in chlorofluorocarbons destroy ozone, O_3, in the upper atmosphere.

There are three main steps in this process.

Step 1   The chlorofluorocarbons are broken down to form free radicals.

$$CCl_3F \rightarrow \bullet CCl_2F + \bullet Cl$$

Step 2   Chlorine radicals react with ozone molecules, breaking them down into oxygen molecules.

Step 3   The reactions in step 2 regenerate the chlorine radicals, so they can go on to destroy more ozone molecules.

(a) Give the names of the three mains steps in this free radical process. **1**

(b) State what provides the energy to break the bonds in chlorofluorocarbons in the upper atmosphere. **1**

(c) State what is meant by the term 'free radical'. **1**

(d) Write a possible equation for step 2. **1**

(e) What is added to cosmetics to prevent similar chain reactions taking place on the skin? **1**